the peach & the coconut

Re-creating the Community of Jesus

simon benham
senior pastor

kerith community church

ACKN OWLE DGEM ENTS

I'd never realised before how big a team it takes to write a book. I'd like to say a huge thank you to everyone involved, but in particular I'd like to thank:

- Penny Lander, who has overseen the whole project and kept it on track with constant encouragement that the end was in sight – it would never have happened without you, Penny.
- Everyone who was kind enough to comment on the early drafts of the book and improve it in so many different ways.
- All the people who were willing to contribute their personal stories – your lives are an inspiration.
- Harriet Evans, our copyeditor, and the whole team at Choir Press who have overseen the production of the book – you have been a joy to work with.
- Mike Charlton, the world's best graphic designer, who took my pages of text and turned them into something beautiful. Mike, I dedicate the chapter on Artists to you.
- My wonderful family, who have had to endure too many occasions where I was typing at my computer trying to finish another chapter when I should have been spending time with them. I love you!
- Jesus, who came into my life when I was eighteen and set me off on the greatest adventure I could ever have imagined. I hope I've accurately reflected the church you want us to be.

Having said all that, I take total ownership of and responsibility for everything I have written. If you don't like it or disagree with it then please hold me completely accountable.

Simon

June 2012

i

KERITH

CHAPTERS

Re-creating the Community of Jesus

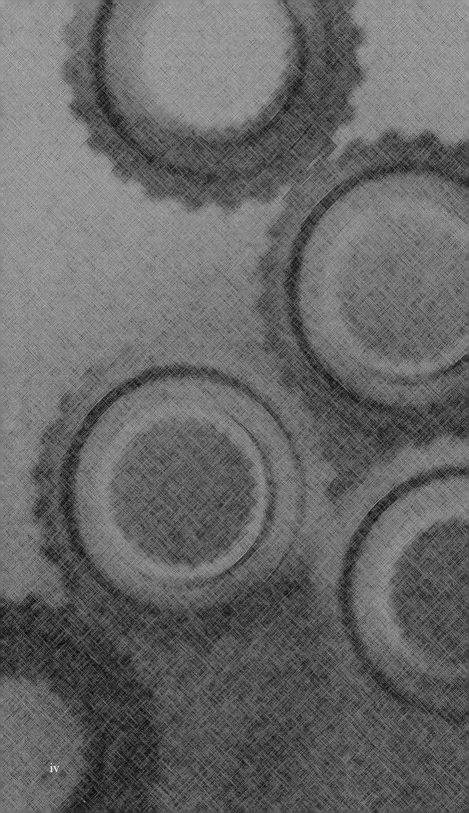

introduction

The Oxford Dictionary defines culture as

" the ideas, customs, and social behaviour of a particular people or society. "

Every family, every town, every football club, every pub, every church, every company and every country has a culture, a particular way in which it behaves and a set of beliefs which drive that behaviour. For a family it might be something as simple as whether meals are eaten at the table or in front of the TV, or who is responsible for putting the rubbish out. Often we're not aware of our culture until it collides with somebody else's. Hence the tension that can arise for a newly married couple as the rubbish begins to pile up and they both sit around waiting for the other person to deal with it, because that was how it was done in the family they grew up in.

Often cultures just develop without anyone thinking too much about them. For instance families develop their own particular way of doing Christmas. You'd probably be hard pressed to work out why one family waits until after lunch before they open all their presents, and another opens them as soon as the day starts. There isn't necessarily any right and wrong about when in the day the presents should be opened, it's just different.

But there are moments where we need to try to define and shape culture, what some have called being 'cultural architects'. We can do that by painting a picture of what we would like the culture to be, and then striving with all our being to build the community we've described.

That's what Martin Luther King Jr did when he stood on the steps of the Lincoln Memorial and delivered his famous 'I Have a Dream' speech. He painted a compelling picture of what American culture might look like if racism ceased to define the cultural boundaries of their society, if people were judged on the quality of their character rather than the colour of their skin, and if everyone was given the same chance to succeed in life. Ultimately that culture was changed to such an extent that Barack Obama could be elected to be President of the United States.

My aim here is to paint a word picture of the culture we want to build in Kerith Community Church, based on a comparison between a peach and a coconut. This isn't so much a description of how things are today (although hopefully we're at least some of the way there) as a picture of where we want to be.

There will always be bits of what we do that don't live up to the ideal, because all of us are messed up, sinful, broken people who bring our messed up, sinful, broken lives into the community. But that must never stop us continuing to strive to build the church that God longs for us to be.

In reading this book you probably fall in to one of three categories:
- You may be thinking about becoming part of our church community
- You may have been part of our church community for a while
- You may be outside our community and just interested in what we do

If you're thinking about becoming part of our church community, this book will hopefully help you decide whether or not this is a community you want to join. We encourage people not to rush that decision. Take time not only to read what's written here, but also to see and experience for yourself what our community is like up close. Join us on a Sunday, go to a Lifegroup, attend a course or join a special interest group (look in the latest LinK magazine or go to the website (www.kerith.co.uk) for details on how to access all of those things). And please ask questions. We love it when people engage with what we're doing enough to question things they don't agree with, or which don't seem to make sense. Maybe we didn't explain it very well, perhaps we need to change what we do and the way we do it, or maybe we just see things differently from you and that isn't going to change. Questions are a great way to clarify which of those it is.

For those of us who have been part of Kerith for a while this book is hopefully a good reminder of the vision we bought into, and can inspire us again to play our unique part in helping make the vision a reality. Vision leaks, and it's important for us to keep restating the vision as clearly as possible in order to keep it fresh and alive. However, it's also important to say that unlike a building, which essentially never changes once the architect has done his design and the building is built, a community is a living organism which constantly needs to change and adapt to the people in it and to the external pressures upon it. Although our core values must never change, if in fifty years' time people are still talking about 'the peach and the coconut' it will probably mean that we've failed to move on, and that what we hoped would be a peach has turned into a coconut. I pray that won't happen!

Finally, if you're reading this as someone outside Kerith Community Church who is simply interested in why we do what we do, I hope you will find this book interesting and informative. I'd encourage you to think about the peach and coconut principles, and how they might apply to your situation. Please feel free to contact us if we could help in any way in making your church or organisation more peachy, or if you'd like to use any of the material in the book in your context.

You'll see that there are three sections to the book. I'd encourage you to read the first eight chapters in the order in which they appear, as they build on each other and set out a framework for every aspect of church life.

They deal with our core beliefs – things like 'who is Jesus?' and 'what did his death on the cross achieve?' The second section covers a whole range of practical issues such as what we think about money or about sex, how we go about resolving conflict, how we value social justice. In the final section we look at our history as a church and our vision for the future.

Although I wrote the first draft of each of these chapters, many different people in our church community then got to review and comment on them. These comments were then incorporated into the text, so that what you're reading here is truly a community effort. We've also included stories from people within our community which hopefully illustrate what we're saying. Some of the names have been changed in order to protect their anonymity.

I hope you enjoy reading "**The Peach and the Coconut**".

At the end of each chapter I'm going to suggest books and other resources which help back up and expand on the ideas which have been covered. Many of the recommended books are available from the Kerith Centre resources area.

The observant amongst you will notice that books which are relevant to more than one chapter are recommended multiple times. I thought that was better than just mentioning them once and hoping you would realise their relevance elsewhere.

For the introduction there is just one suggested resource.

An Unstoppable Force
Erwin Raphael McManus

This book first introduced me to the idea and the importance of cultural architects. Erwin was also the first person I ever heard use the image of the peach as the sort of church we should aspire to be.

O N E

ONE

Exploring the Community of Jesus

coconuts

> When one of the Pharisees invited Jesus to have dinner with him, he went to the Pharisee's house and reclined at the table. A woman in that town who lived a sinful life learned that Jesus was eating at the Pharisee's house, so she came there with an alabaster jar of perfume. As she stood behind him at his feet weeping, she began to wet his feet with her tears. Then she wiped them with her hair, kissed them and poured perfume on them.
> When the Pharisee who had invited him saw this, he said to himself, 'If this man were a prophet, he would know who is touching him and what kind of woman she is - that she is a sinner.'
>
> **(Luke 7:36-39)**

I remember as a child visiting the village fête, where one of the stalls would always be a coconut shy. All the lads would line up for a go, wanting to impress people (particularly the girls) with the strength and accuracy of their throw. I was never too great in either department, but given enough money would usually manage to win at least one coconut.

Having got a coconut, the question would then arise as to what to do with the prize. There would normally be a bit of shaking, just to check that it was a 'proper' one with milk inside, and then would start the quest to get to the hidden treasures within. First would come an attempt to extract the milk. That involved getting out Dad's hand drill and attempting to drill out the eyes of the coconut whilst holding it between the legs (always a risky exercise almost guaranteed to produce holes in the trousers and wounds in the legs).

We'd get to pour the milk out into a cup, complete with bits of the shell. The little bit we tasted would always be pretty undrinkable.

Then it was back to the tool box for a hammer to try to smash the coconut in two. Once that was achieved the result would be similarly disappointing.

Coconut might be OK when wrapped in milk chocolate in the middle of a Bounty, or in a Peshwari naan with a nice curry, but raw it's just not that nice (apologies to any raw coconut lovers out there). Now with the coconut in bits it would be hung up on a piece of string in the garden for the birds to eat. They always seemed to be about as keen on coconut as I was. Then after a month or two of shrivelling in the wind and the rain it would go to its final resting place, the bin.

The coconut represents one model for a community. A community which is hard to get into, hard to penetrate, and when you do get in it turns out to be a disappointment.

Jesus constantly found himself coming up against a coconut community led by the religious rulers of his time, the very people who were supposed to be making it easy for people to find God. He described their community this way:

"Woe to you, teachers of the law and Pharisees, you hypocrites! You are like whitewashed tombs, which look beautiful on the outside but on the inside are full of the bones of the dead and everything unclean." (Matthew 23:27)

In this description of a coconut community Jesus goes beyond saying that it is just hollow. He makes two penetrating observations about what is on the inside of these communities.

Firstly they are full of dead men's bones. Dead bones represent a structure which used to support life and have meaning, but which has now ceased to serve the purpose for which it was created. Coconut communities can often be filled with activity, but it is activity which, although it may once have had life and relevance, is now dead and meaningless. If a community is to remain relevant then it needs to be constantly dealing with the 'dead bones' or else it might quickly turn into a coconut. We need to cling to tradition which flows from following the Bible, but move on from tradition which just flows out of 'that's the way we've always done it'.

Secondly Jesus says that coconut communities are full of everything unclean. He is saying this to the Pharisees who considered themselves to be the cleanest of the clean, but who in their desire to become clean had become hard hearted, judgemental, unforgiving, unloving, uncaring and self righteous. This sort of hypocrisy can often lie at the core of coconut communities, because they embody an ideology which could be described as:

BEHAVE → BELIEVE → BELONG

This ideology says that before you can experience what it is to be part of the community you first of all need to behave in the way the community dictates, to live the right sort of life externally, only associate with the right sort of people, even wear the right sort of clothes and have the right sort of job. Then if you pass the behaviour test you need to have the right set of beliefs, to have your understanding of what to believe about God and the Bible in line with that of everyone else in the community. Only if you pass those tests can you belong and really be a part of the community.

It's so easy to become self righteous in a community like that, convinced that because you stick to the rules and believe the right things you are better than all the people around. That was certainly true of the Pharisees. But it is also easy to become a community of mask wearers (which was the original meaning of the word hypocrite), because people are unwilling to own up to their struggles and any doubts that they might have for fear of being cut off from the community. Instead people pretend and cover up, internally struggling with life issues and questions about their faith without ever finding a safe place to own up to them, talk them through and get help, input, or even just reassurance that other people struggle with the same thing.

It is also very hard for anyone from outside to join a community like this, because they have to sort out their behaviour and their beliefs before they can belong. It's highly unlikely that people with different lifestyles and beliefs are ever going to feel anything but indifference or even rejection from a coconut community, even if that community genuinely believes it is trying to reach out to and love the people around it.

I once heard someone describe the expectation of coconut communities as being like a fisherman who expects to catch fish which have already been cleaned up, had the head and tail removed, been filleted and coated in breadcrumbs to turn them into fish fingers. When Jesus called us to fish for people,[1] his expectation was that there would still be much work to do on the fish once they'd been caught, lots of believing and behaving still to be worked out.

My observation is that over time, and without a community of cultural architects to keep the vision alive, communities can so easily revert to coconut behaviour. That can even happen to the best and most godly people.

Consider how Peter slipped into coconut behaviour. We read early on in the book of Acts that he had a direct revelation from God that it was now all right for Jewish believers to eat any food.[2] And he was the first person to see a breakthrough in God saving non-Jews.[3] Yet several chapters later we read that within a few years Peter had to be faced up to by Paul for having slipped back into exclusivity and only eating with fellow Jews. [4] (Note that it was Paul's grasp of the core of the gospel which allowed him to challenge Peter so strongly and be a cultural architect in this situation.) If it can happen to Peter then it can happen to any of us.

....

I haven't found too many books which focus on coconut communities (nor would I want any of us to spend too much time dwelling on them). However, I would encourage you to spend time reading through the gospels and make note of the interactions which Jesus has with the

SUGGESTED RESOURCES

Pharisees, particularly those where somebody else is involved too. Here are a few suggestions:

Matthew 9:1-8
forgiving & healing a paralysed man
Matthew 9:32-34
healing a mute man
Matthew 12:9-14
healing on the Sabbath
Matthew 15:1-20 & Mark 7:1-23
following tradition instead of God's command
Mark 11:27-33
questioning Jesus' authority

Mark 12:13-17
paying taxes
Luke 5:27-32
eating with tax collectors and sinners
Luke 7:36-50
forgiving a sinful woman
Luke 10:25-37
parable of the Good Samaritan
John 8:1-11
woman caught in adultery

peaches

Jesus straightened up and asked her,
'Woman, where are they?
Has no one condemned you?'
'No one, sir,' she said.
'Then neither do I condemn you,' Jesus declared.
'Go now and leave your life of sin.'

(John 8:10–11)

That's enough about coconuts. Let's move on to thinking about how a peach community differs from what we've just described.

There are two qualities of a peach which I'd like us to think about.

SOFT ON THE OUTSIDE

A peach is very easy to get into. The skin doesn't offer much resistance to anything. Several times when I've spoken on the peach and the coconut I've brought along one of each for a visual demonstration. More than once I've carried them in my soft shoulder bag, and although the coconut has invariably survived the journey intact I've often needed to make a last minute phone call home for a peach replacement (for this reason I now have an artificial peach!). That's just what peaches are like. At least an apple gives a bit of resistance, a banana has a skin which protects it, but a peach is just so easy to get into.

That was certainly what the community of Jesus looked like from the vantage point of the Pharisees. They couldn't understand the company he kept and the people he associated with – the very people they wanted to hold at arm's length and have nothing to do with. Jesus is very relaxed spending time with the woman at the well (a Samaritan, a woman and a multiple divorcee), [5] Zacchaeus the tax collector (who was stealing money from his fellow Jews and collaborating with the Roman army),[6] a blind beggar who got told to be quiet because he was shouting out to Jesus so loudly,[7] a leper whom no one else wanted to touch but Jesus reached out and embraced[8] and the prostitute who washed his feet,[9] or just turning up at weddings and parties.[10] One of the greatest accusations the Pharisees made against Jesus was that he was 'a friend of tax collectors and "sinners"'. In their eyes Jesus was very soft with the people he allowed into his world. He was utterly comfortable around these people, and they were comfortable being around him. There was no need in the eyes of Jesus to behave or believe before you could belong, before you could experience what it was to spend time with him.

Timothy Keller speaks powerfully on this in his book The Prodigal God, which is based on the story of the prodigal (or 'lost') son found in Luke 15:11–32. In a chapter entitled 'The People Around Jesus' Timothy contrasts 'younger brothers' (people who engage in wild living and reject the traditional morality of their societies) and 'older brothers' (the religious – in Jesus' case the Pharisees and teachers of the law). He says:

> Jesus' teaching consistently attracted the irreligious while offending the Bible-believing, religious people of his day. However, in the main our churches do not have this effect. The kind of outsiders Jesus attracted are not attracted to contemporary churches, even our most avant-garde ones. We tend to draw conservative, buttoned down, moralising people. The licentious and liberated or the broken and marginal avoid church. That can only mean one thing. If the preaching of our ministers and the practice of our parishioners do not have the same effect that Jesus had, then we must not be declaring the message that Jesus did. If our churches aren't appealing to younger brothers, they may be more full of elder brothers than we'd like to think. [11]

We can produce churches which are growing, influential, well funded, planting other churches, even being applauded by other churches and society. But if we want to be sure that we are declaring the message that Jesus declared, we need to ask the question 'are we attracting the sort of people who were attracted to Jesus?'

As we've already seen, coconut communities are characterised by the progression:

Peach communities totally reverse this flow, to become:

That's what happened in the community of Jesus. People felt free to belong in his company, then in that environment something happened in relation to their beliefs, then that change in belief began to change their behaviour.

Consider the example of Zacchaeus, the chief tax collector whom we meet in Luke 19. Jesus invites himself into Zacchaeus' home, a move which provokes the response 'All the people saw this and began to mutter, "He has gone to be the guest of a sinner"'.[12] Then as Jesus spends time with him in his home something changes in Zacchaeus' belief system. He goes from being someone who just wanted to get a glimpse of Jesus as he was passing through town to addressing him as 'Lord'. Then something changes in his behaviour – something far more dramatic than anything a community which simply has a set of rules and regulations could hope to produce. Zacchaeus gives half of his possessions to the poor and pays back four times what he has cheated anyone of. He's not doing this out of compulsion or under duress but because he's had a change of heart.

That's the miracle which I believe can take place in a peach community. Not that we can change anyone, but we can create the environment, the atmosphere, the soil if you like, where God can get hold of people and perform a miracle in their lives.

But let us recognise from the start that building the community of the peach isn't simple or straightforward. Anyone who has ever eaten a peach also knows it can be an incredibly messy experience. It's not the sort of thing you want to be found doing in public as inevitably the juice ends up all over your face and running down your clothes. It was like that for Jesus too. There was something very messy about getting involved in these people's lives. They didn't have it all together, many of them were very much a work in progress and he took lots of criticism for his friendships with them, yet Jesus loved being around these people.

There are also no guarantees that people will change. Coconut communities maintain their purity by only allowing in people who have already made the grade, who are already living up to the standards. What stops a peach community from becoming indistinguishable from the people around it?

SOLID AT THE CORE

It's important to note that a peach isn't soft all the way through. At its core is a stone, and if you bite the stone you're likely to do yourself some damage.

Jesus never once compromised on his core. Take the woman caught having sex with a guy she wasn't married to. [13] The Pharisees in this situation had no interest in the woman; they just wanted to use her brokenness to try to catch Jesus out. Jesus, in contrast, took a genuine

interest in her as an individual, telling her that he didn't condemn her but then going on to tell her to leave her old sinful lifestyle behind. Jesus was willing first to love her just as she was, but then loved her to such an extent that he wasn't willing to leave her in that state. In the words of John Burke, 'come as you are, but don't stay that way'.[14]

We want to be as clear about the core as Jesus was. We never want to compromise or seek to hide what exists at our core, the truth about Jesus Christ and what his life and death represent, and what it means to follow him with all of our heart, mind, soul and strength. Those truths don't always sit comfortably with the society we live in, but that makes it all the more important that we're clear about them and never give in to the temptation to fudge them or compromise our core beliefs.

But we also need to be clear about what is core truth and what is just tradition or a particular view on how church should be done.

Truth is unchanging, but traditions and ways of doing church always need to be challenged, and when necessary changed.

PEACHES NOT TOMATOES

The danger with being soft on the outside as a community is that we might become soft all the way through – more of a tomato than a peach. Without cultural and spiritual architects, elders, key leaders and community influencers who will keep restating and redirecting the community back to its core values, my observation is that communities naturally gravitate towards one of two extremes. They either become more like a coconut, hard on the outside but dead on the inside, or more like tomatoes, soft all the way through. In Christian terms that might be expressed as being either more conservative or more liberal. Conservatives are passionate about being theologically correct but can miss out on loving people in the process. Liberals are passionate about loving people but can end up compromising or ignoring bits of the Bible which could cause conflict, ridicule or offence. Jesus was able to be culturally liberal on the outside and yet theologically conservative at his core, in short he was peachy.

And it wasn't just Jesus who seemed to reach for that ideal. Paul could never be described as compromising his core beliefs (take a look at Galatians chapters 1 and 2 for an example of how solid he was at his core), and yet on the outside he seemed to be incredibly peachy in wanting to remove all external barriers to people far from God hearing this incredible message. Just consider his words in 1 Corinthians 9: 'I have become all things to all people so that by all possible means I might save some'. [15] Or his appeal on Mars Hill where he quotes from their pagan poets and philosophers. [16] Or his desire to think long and hard about speaking in tongues in church if it was going to alienate and confuse non-believers. [17]

We're not the first people down this road, nor will we be the last. In fact I believe it is the job of every generation to define what peachiness looks like in their cultural context. This is our attempt to do that for our generation. So please join me as we take a journey into what it means for us to build the community of the peach.

No Perfect People Allowed
John Burke

When we first came across this book we were well down the road of trying to build a more peachy community, but this book helped us greatly as many issues addressed in the book

were the issues we found we were facing. Although it doesn't anywhere use the language of peaches and coconuts, the church which John Burke describes is very much the church we are trying to build.

The Prodigal God
Timothy Keller

Tim Keller shows from the story of the prodigal son that older brothers (the religious) can be as far from God as their younger brothers (the 'sinful'), but that God loves both in equal measure. Again, although it doesn't use the language of peaches and coconuts, it wrestles with many of the same ideas and underlying attitudes.

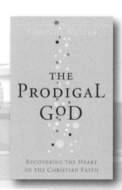

core

> **For God so loved the world that he gave his one and only Son, that whoever believes in him shall not perish but have eternal life.**
>
> **(John 3:16)**

At the core of our culture and everything we seek to do as a church is Jesus, and the incredible message of good news which is wrapped up in his life, death and resurrection. I'm going to summarise what is at our core using five words:

LOVE

EVIL

RESCUE

CHOICE   RESTORE

LOVE

At the core of all we are as a community is a God of love. Not a God who is uninterested in all that goes on in the world, or a God who is constantly angry with us and needs to be avoided or appeased, but a God who is primarily characterised as a God of love. This God of love is a God who created us for his pleasure, created us for relationship with him and whose ultimate aim is that we will be able to enjoy being with him for all eternity.

EVIL

In his love for us God chose to give us free will, meaning that he gave us the ability to choose whether or not we wanted to love him. The Bible tells us that although God created a perfect world, evil entered the world when Adam and Eve used their free will to disobey God in the garden of Eden.[18] The impact of their disobedience, which the Bible calls sin, was catastrophic, with multiple relationships falling apart. Their relationship with God (theology), their inner relationship (psychology), their relationship with one another (sociology) and their relationship with their environment (ecology) were all irrevocably affected for the worse.

We all live with the fall-out from those broken relationships; they are evident everywhere you look in the world today. We would like to believe that we can fix these problems ourselves, but the difficulty is that at the root of all our problems is our broken relationship with God, and the only way to fix that is to live a sin-free life, which none of us has the ability to do. Without dealing with our broken relationship with God, none of the other problems can possibly be addressed, and evil will continue to rule and to grow.

The ultimate consequence of our decision to go our own way will be that God will love us so much that he will allow us to have what we have chosen, an eternity without him. The Bible calls that place set aside by God, the place which is totally devoid of his presence, 'hell', and tells us that it is a place of eternal torment and pain.

RESCUE

John 3:16 makes it clear that God, out of his love for us, has chosen not to leave us in our messed up state, on our way to hell, but to make a way for us to get back to the relationship God originally created us for.

The Bible tells us that God's rescue plan was to send his son, Jesus, born as a baby to Mary, a virgin. Jesus was both fully man and fully God. He lived the perfect life we could never live, and then died on the cross. On the cross he paid the penalty for our sin, taking on himself God's wrath and anger at sin. The result is he has now made a way for us to be forgiven, washed clean of all our sin, be in right relationship with God and be adopted into his family. Three days later Jesus was raised from the dead, showing that death had been defeated and could no longer hold him, and opening up to us a new life, not just forgiven but as new creations, with the same power which raised Jesus from the dead now available to each one of us. He then returned to heaven, sending the Holy Spirit to be with us in his place. One day he will come again to judge the world and to establish a new heaven and a new earth where we will be with God for eternity.

We all love rescue stories. Whether it's lifeboat men rescuing people from a sinking ship, the drama of tunnels being dug to rescue Chilean miners or Woody being rescued by the other toys in Toy Story 2, they resonate deeply with something in the human spirit. As we read the Bible we realise that this is the ultimate rescue story. Once evil has entered the world, the whole of the Bible is about God's plan to rescue mankind, and we are the ones in need of a rescuer, in need of a saviour.

CHOICE

Jesus' death now gives us a choice that we never had before, the option of choosing to step back into a relationship with this God of love. That choice means deciding to:

Accept that you've messed up... you're a sinner, and that you need a saviour. That there is nothing you can do to deal with, to atone for, your own sin. That your only hope is to believe in Jesus who has died in your place for your sin (what the theologians call 'substitutionary atonement').

Believe that Jesus was who he said he was... that he died for your sin. That your attempts at self-atonement are hopeless, and that God now freely offers you his forgiveness as a gift which you have done nothing to deserve or to earn (what the Bible calls 'grace').

Consider that although the gift will cost you nothing... working out that gift in your life will cost you everything. It means making Jesus Lord of your life. Giving all you are to him – your life choices, your relationships, your finances, your reputation. Putting all of it under his control, believing and trusting that he has a plan for your life far better than the one you could ever come up with. That's a huge decision to make, and not one which should ever be taken lightly.

Decide to follow Jesus. The Bible uses the word 'repentance', which means to stop living life your way and to turn around and start living it God's way. Jesus now says:
'Here I am! I stand at the door and knock. If anyone hears my voice and opens the door, I will come in and eat with that person, and they with me.' [19]

If you're not yet a follower of Jesus Christ then right now you can open that door to start a relationship with him.

And when you make that choice you make an amazing discovery. You find that although it might seem to you as though you chose God, there is another heavenly perspective which is that God chose you first. In John 15:16 Jesus says 'You did not choose me, but I chose you'. Paul writes to the church in Ephesus that 'he chose us in him before the creation of the world to be holy and blameless in his sight.'[20] We can take great confidence and assurance from this perspective that it is God who has chosen to make us part of his family, and that as adopted children we can never lose our salvation or our relationship with him.

RESTORE

God's purpose was not just that a few individuals would be saved, but that the whole of creation would be restored to its original purpose.

As followers of Jesus Christ, we are now in the restoration business, helping other people far from God to find a relationship with him and working out God's heart for justice in the world we live in, God's heart for the poor, the hungry and the fatherless.

Jesus expresses that heart for restoration when he teaches us to pray 'Your kingdom come, your will be done, on earth as it is in heaven'. [21] His desire is that we would be a part of bringing some of heaven to earth.

CLEAR ON THE CORE

Jesus was very clear on the core of who he was and what he believed. As we'll see in the chapter on grace and truth, one of his catchphrases was 'I tell you the truth'. He was never scared to declare truth, even when it was uncomfortable or caused people to leave him. As a peach community we want to have a similar clarity about what is at our core, never compromising it or being vague about who God is and what we believe about him.

WHAT'S NEXT?

Perhaps having read this you've realised that you're not yet a follower of Jesus Christ. If so you stand on the edge of the best decision you will ever make. As Peter declared on the day of Pentecost when he was asked the question 'what must we do to be saved?':

Repent and be baptised, every one of you, in the name of Jesus Christ for the forgiveness of

your sins. And you will receive the gift of the Holy Spirit. The promise is for you and your children and for all who are far off—for all whom the Lord our God will call. (Acts 2:38–39)

Right now you can repent and turn to God. If you haven't done so already please consider making what for me was the best choice I have ever made.

Or perhaps as you read this you've realised you've been half-hearted in following Jesus. Half-hearted in your commitment and longing for him. Well, take this opportunity to repent, to rediscover your first love and to get on board with God's plan for your life. If you're not in one already, find a Bible-believing, God-filled local church and start living for him.

Vintage Jesus
Mark Driscoll and Gerry Breshears

You'd struggle to find a clearer statement of all that is core about Jesus, and what we believe about

SUGGESTED RESOURCES

him, than that contained in this book. I thoroughly recommend it.

The Alpha Course

Alpha provides a safe place for anyone wanting to explore and think more about what it means to have a relationship with Jesus. Every session of the ten-week course has either a meal or refreshments, a talk on some aspect of the Christian faith and then an opportunity to discuss the talk. We run both daytime and evening courses twice a year – see our website, or the Alpha website at http://uk-england.alpha.org/ for more details.

The Lion, the Witch and the Wardrobe
C.S. Lewis

The story of Aslan the lion, who represents Jesus and who willingly lays down his life for the people he loves. This story, and the others in the Narnia series, helped me get a fresh perspective on Jesus and his rescue mission.

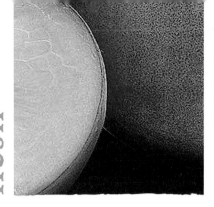

flesh

For God so loved the world that he gave his one and only Son, that whoever believes in him shall not perish but have eternal life. For God did not send his Son into the world to condemn the world, but to save the world through him.

(John 3:16–17)

We've looked at the core – the solid stone at the centre of a peach. Now for the juicy, edible part – the flesh. It's the outer flesh which is inviting and easy to bite into, not off-putting and hard like the shell of a coconut. What does the flesh look like for that sort of community – one that Jesus would build?

John 3:16 is often named as the most popular or the most well known verse in the Bible. That's not surprising, given that as we saw in the last chapter it describes the core of the Christian faith.

But not so many people make it on to the next verse, verse 17. I personally think that's a huge loss, as verse 17 explains so much of the context for how God wanted the message of verse 16 to be expressed. That the message Jesus came to bring was not one of condemnation and shame but one of salvation and hope.

Ever since I first read it I've been haunted by a story Philip Yancey tells at the start of his outstanding book What's So Amazing About Grace?:

A prostitute came to me in wretched straits, homeless, sick, unable to buy food for her two-year-old daughter. Through sobs and tears, she told me she had been renting out her daughter — two years old! — to men interested in kinky sex. She made more renting out her daughter for an hour than she could earn on her own in a night. She had to do it, she said, to support her own drug habit. I could hardly bear hearing her sordid story...

At last I asked if she had ever thought of going to a church for help. I will never forget the look of pure, naive shock that crossed her face. 'Church!' she cried. 'Why would I ever go there? I was already feeling terrible about myself. They'd just make me feel worse.' [22]

Why is it that women like this prostitute rushed towards Jesus, yet would never dream of going anywhere near most churches? It was because in Jesus they found not condemnation but love, and the impact of that love was that they came to love him too. Let's take a look at a few of those people from the life of Jesus.

We've already talked about Zacchaeus, a despised tax collector who has the shock of Jesus inviting himself into his home. Jesus follows up on Zacchaeus' public declaration to make good on everyone he has cheated by saying:

Today salvation has come to this house, because this man, too, is a son of Abraham. For the Son of Man came to seek and to save the lost. (Luke 19:9–10)

John 3:17 has been fulfilled in Zacchaeus' life. Rather than condemnation he has found salvation. Jesus' rescue mission has been successful.

We first meet Nicodemus in John 3 when he comes to Jesus in the middle of the night. Nicodemus is part of the ruling Jewish authorities, the people who will ultimately put Jesus to death. He's clearly intrigued by Jesus. It's not obvious whether he comes at night because he is scared to be seen with Jesus or simply because that's the only time he can get access to him, but what is clear is the way Jesus treats Nicodemus. He gives him time, answers his questions and treats him with dignity and respect, even though he's part of the group who Jesus knows are ultimately going to put him to death, one of the coconuts. Note also though that Jesus isn't afraid to challenge him to 'come into the light'. [23]

It's interesting that nothing seems to change with Nicodemus. He doesn't immediately leave the Pharisees and join the disciples or experience any obvious dramatic life transformation. We are often so disappointed when we feel as though we've had a 'good conversation' with someone who then seems to show no interest. I think Jesus has a much deeper confidence in the power of God to change people.

We meet Nicodemus twice more. In John 7:50 we hear him arguing with his fellow Pharisees in defence of Jesus. Then in John 19:38–40 we see Nicodemus, with Joseph of Arimathea, publicly identifying with Jesus after his crucifixion by preparing his body for burial. All of that flowed out of that conversation with Jesus three years earlier, a conversation filled with grace and truth.

THE WOMAN AT THE WELL

The next person Jesus meets couldn't be a bigger contrast to Nicodemus. In John 4 we read how Jesus goes on a journey with his disciples, and on the way meets a Samaritan woman at a well. This woman has been married five times, and is now living with a man she isn't married to.

All the customs of the day say Jesus should have nothing to do with her – she's a woman, she has an immoral lifestyle and she is a Samaritan. There were as many reasons for Jesus to reject her as for us to reject the woman in Philip Yancey's story.

Yet the response of Jesus is anything but rejection. He asks her for a drink of water, what could be more natural than that, and speaks to her simply as one human being interacting with another. He again answers her questions with dignity and respect. And get this: even though he knows all about her immoral past, he doesn't once tell her that before she can get into a relationship with God she needs to sort out her living arrangements. He realises that before God deals with her external behaviour he wants to deal with her inner brokenness and spiritual thirst for a faith which is real.

Unlike Nicodemus the impact on this woman's life is much more immediate. She goes back to her town and brings a huge crowd out to meet this Jesus, and through her many people come to believe in Jesus in this most unlikely of places.

And it all started with Jesus treating this broken woman with love and with grace.

The final picture of peachiness we're going to look at is the sinful woman who washed Jesus' feet. We find it in Luke 7:36–50. Here is the opening of the story:

WASHING JESUS' FEET

When one of the Pharisees invited Jesus to have dinner with him, he went to the Pharisee's house and reclined at the table. A woman in that town who lived a sinful life learned that Jesus was eating at the Pharisee's house, so she came there with an alabaster jar of perfume. As she stood behind him at his feet weeping, she began to wet his feet with her tears. Then she wiped them with her hair, kissed them and poured perfume on them.

When the Pharisee who had invited him saw this, he said to himself, 'If this man were a prophet, he would know who is touching him and what kind of woman she is—that she is a sinner.' (Luke 7:36–39)

We see here a collision between the coconut world of Simon the Pharisee and the peachy world of Jesus. I've got tears in my eyes as I reflect on this woman and the way Jesus treats her. The risk she took as she entered the home of this Pharisee, intent on offering her act of worship to Jesus but fearing rejection, not only the rejection she must have experienced all of her life, but possible rejection from Jesus as well. And what it must have communicated to her as Jesus allowed her to wash his feet with her tears, wipe them with her hair, kiss them and pour perfume on them. The love, the acceptance, the mercy, the forgiveness of all her mistakes, the hope that her future could be different from her past. How Jesus must have enjoyed saying to her: **Your faith has saved you; go in peace. (Luke 7:50)**

MISSION ACCOMPLISHED!

Yet notice also how Jesus treats Simon. Not only is Jesus willing to come into Simon's home, but when Simon in his heart condemns both Jesus and the woman for what goes on, Jesus tells him a story to demonstrate the hardness of Simon's heart and to try to win him too. Just feast your eyes on how Jesus deals with Simon:

When the Pharisee who had invited him saw this, he said to himself, 'If this man were a prophet, he would know who is touching him and what kind of woman she is—that she is a sinner.'

Jesus answered him, 'Simon, I have something to tell you.'

'Tell me, teacher,' he said.

'Two people owed money to a certain moneylender. One owed him five hundred denarii, and the other fifty. Neither of them had the money to pay him back, so he forgave the debts of both. Now which of them will love him more?'

Simon replied, 'I suppose the one who had the bigger debt forgiven.'

'You have judged correctly,' Jesus said. (Luke 7:39–43)

Jesus is as passionate about reaching Simon as he is about the woman.

THE BODY OF CHRIST

In 1 Corinthians 12:27 Paul tells us:

'you are the body of Christ, and each one of you is a part of it'.

As the body of Christ on the earth today, as his hands and his feet, his voice and his heart in the world today, we need to impact people in the same way Jesus did. That means the church being a place which proclaims not just the truth of Jesus, but his love too.

There is so much more I could say about the church being the flesh of the peach. About us being loving, accepting, welcoming, friendly, interested in people, willing to step out of our comfort zones, willing to be criticised by the religious for our love of people far from God. But rather than hearing me say any more, please take time to think about how Jesus so wonderfully modelled all those things, and dare to imagine for a moment a church, a community of God's people, which would truly be the body of Christ on the earth today.

....

What's So Amazing About Grace?
Philip Yancey

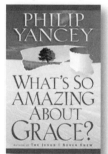

SUGGESTED RESOURCES

This book changed my understanding of Jesus more than any other that I've read (other than the Bible). Seeing how grace worked itself out in the life of Jesus transformed my view of him for ever.

No Perfect People Allowed
John Burke

John deals so well with how we reach out to and love people who might expect to find condemnation and judgement in a church environment.

KHADIJEH

I was born into a very religious Muslim family. As I was growing up my father used force as a form of discipline. There was never any love, trust or respect. I was never told that I was loved or special and my life was full of misery. I remember praying to God to make me a Christian, as I had seen the other children at school have happy lives, and thought the only way I could be saved from this life was to become a Christian.

When I got to college I found boys. Looking back, I realise I was trying to find the love I never got from my parents. On my first week of uni my father died of cancer and I couldn't live at home any more. I moved out, lost my faith, and my involvement with boys became a self-destructive spiral.

When I needed a lifeline, a year later, I met the most amazing man, Michael. The moment I met him I knew he was special and he was nothing like the boys I had been involved with. We started talking and as I got to know him more, I started to really like him.

At this point in time I didn't believe in 'love' and thought it was a concept used by boys to get girls. The only God I knew was the God I had been taught about. All I felt was guilt about moving away from God and guilt for all my sins. I was overwhelmed. Michael helped me through all this guilt by showing me love and that God loved me.

We knew very early on that we were made for each other but that we could only get married if our foundations were the same. So I started to read about Christianity. The more I read the more confused I got with the logic of Christianity and the logic of Islam. A year and a half into our relationship Michael took me to a Christian camp, Momentum. There I saw Christians just being real. I had been to church before but this was completely different. It was amazing, but I was still cynical.

For most of our relationship, every time we approached the subject of religion we argued. It was easier to ignore it, understanding that we both believed in God, and to get on with our lives.

We moved to Bracknell in January 2010 and Michael suggested that we find a church. We came across Kerith Community Church. I had visited quite a few churches throughout my journey; I found Kerith to be very welcoming and inviting. The services are very much rooted in solid Bible teaching, which is really important for me. I love the way that even though it is such a big church the ministry team can still interact with the people like a family. I felt people were open and I could be myself and no one judged me. Even before I became a Christian I could feel God lived in this church. One Sunday, one of the elders prophesied over us and told us that it was in God's plan for us to have met and then to get married, which was a big relief to us as it reaffirmed that we were meant to be together.

Just over three and a half years into our relationship, we went to Momentum again and this time I had an incredible encounter with God. I felt as though my heart was taken out and put back all clean. When God returned my heart to me I felt his presence wash over me, I felt his love and grace, my pain turned into joy and my tears turned into those of pure happiness and peace. I gave my life to Christ. Then in 2012 Michael and I were finally married at the Kerith Centre.
My prayers have been answered!

grace
& truth

> **The Word became flesh and made his dwelling among us. We have seen his glory, the glory of the one and only Son, who came from the Father, full of grace and truth.**
>
> **(John 1:14)**

One of my prayers for this book was that it (and I) would be true to what the Bible teaches. I remember that in my early days of being a Christian I'd often get an idea for something to talk about at a Bible study or in a small group I was leading, and then try to find verses and Bible stories which would back up my point of view. Very annoyingly there were many occasions when I found the Bible didn't say what I wanted it to!

Leading a small group wasn't too much of a problem, as there were lots of more experienced Christians around to put me right. In leading a church being true to the Bible is far more crucial, as the potential is there to lead a whole community down a blind alley, or even into heresy.

So is the concept of God wanting us to be a peach-like community really biblical? It might be a nice concept, but that's not enough if we want to build our community and our culture around this idea.

I realise that if you search the Bible for the word 'peach' you won't find it anywhere (you won't find coconut either – I just tried). But the concept of being peachy, soft on the outside but solid at the core, is one which is rooted in the very character of God. John tells us that Jesus was 'full of grace and truth', which fully encompasses all the ideas wrapped up in our longing to be a peach community.

TRUTH

We live in an age which would like to believe that everyone can have their own version of truth, and that as long as you sincerely believe whatever it is you believe then that is truth for you, even if it makes no sense to anyone else. We're encouraged to think that all religions lead to God, that there are no moral absolutes, and that anyone who says anything different is narrow and intolerant, bigoted and arrogant.

Yet Jesus, whom many would see as a great moral teacher, took a very different approach to truth. Consider these words:

> I am the way, the truth and the life.
> No one comes to the Father except through me.
> (John 14:6)

Go back and read that again. Let the full impact of Jesus' clarity speak to you. There's nothing vague or fuzzy about a statement like that, or any sense that you can define your own version of truth. Jesus was very clear that he's the only way to get to God the Father – no 'all ways lead to God' there. Seventy-eight times in the gospels Jesus is recorded using the phrase 'I tell you the truth' when talking to the disciples or the crowds. It seemed to be one of his catchphrases. He was never vague or apologetic about truth.

If we are to be the body of Christ on the earth today then we must have the same confidence in truth – confidence in the truth of the gospel, in the truth that Jesus is the only way to God, and in the truths the Bible speaks about sin and the way to be set free.

BUT NOT TRUTH ALONE

Truth on its own can be a horrible thing. Some people use truth like a wrecking ball used to demolish buildings, using truth to condemn, destroy and knock people down. That was how the Pharisees used truth against the woman caught in the act of adultery whom we meet in John 8. They were absolutely correct in their analysis of her sinful lifestyle, but being full of truth led to them wanting to stone her to death.

Truth on its own, knowing you are right and others are wrong, can result in an arrogant, critical, condemnatory, judgemental and superior spirit. Yet Jesus, who was full of truth, never once acted in any of those ways towards the people he met.

God's heart has never been to destroy, as truth on its own can do, but to restore.

GRACE AND TRUTH IN ACTION

Many of the examples of peach behaviour we've looked at relate to how we treat people outside the church community. But how does the idea of the peach, this combination of grace and truth, apply when it comes to people within our community, and particularly those who fail? Being a peach community doesn't just affect how we treat outsiders. It should also have a huge impact on how we treat people within our community when they mess up. Yet so often that doesn't seem to happen in church life. I've seen too many situations where Christians who have undeniably messed up have consequently been rejected and condemned by people within their church, their denomination or their movement. It sometimes seems easier to express grace to people outside the community than within it.

One of the most remarkable grace stories is that of David when he committed adultery with Bathsheba. Let's review the story (you can read it in full in 2 Samuel 11 and 12).

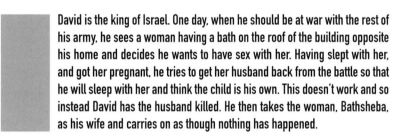

David is the king of Israel. One day, when he should be at war with the rest of his army, he sees a woman having a bath on the roof of the building opposite his home and decides he wants to have sex with her. Having slept with her, and got her pregnant, he tries to get her husband back from the battle so that he will sleep with her and think the child is his own. This doesn't work and so instead David has the husband killed. He then takes the woman, Bathsheba, as his wife and carries on as though nothing has happened.

Let's stop it there. David had replaced Saul, who lost the kingship because he didn't lead in the way God wanted him to. Surely now this is going to be the end of the road for David; God is going to choose a new king. But what we discover is that God is a God of the second chance. He faces David with the truth by sending a man called Nathan to speak to him. But God inspires Nathan not just to face him bluntly with the facts, but to present those facts in such a compelling way that David is able to grasp the seriousness of what he has done. Nathan isn't there just as a purveyor of truth, some sort of moral arbiter to pronounce God's judgement over David and his sin. Instead God's heart, expressed through Nathan, is to restore David and give him that second chance.

Psalm 51 records David's response. We see his recognition of his sinfulness, his prayer for forgiveness and desire for cleansing. There is a clear recognition of his own brokenness, asking God to give him a new heart and to use him to continue to turn others back to God. Nathan's presentation of the truth achieves what it was intended to do.

Let's not miss the fact that there were consequences for David's sin. The child born from the affair dies, and David is told there will continue to be conflict in his family as a result of his affair. We are told one of his sons rapes his sister and destroys her life and is later murdered by another son.

There will always be consequences for sin; people may live the rest of their lives dealing with the fall-out from what they have done. But there is a huge difference between living with that fall-out when you have been forgiven and accepted back into a community willing to give you a second chance, and living with the consequences of sin far from God and cut off by the community.

We see that again in Peter's denial of Jesus. Peter was the one over whom Jesus had declared 'you are Peter, and on this rock I will build my church'.[24] But then he fails spectacularly when he denies Jesus three times. Yet when Jesus meets Peter again after his resurrection, his whole heart is to restore Peter, not just in terms of their relationship but also of Peter's key role within the fledgling church.[25]

People will mess up and fail within the community of the peach. We must never expect sinless perfection from one another. If we do then we're just fooling ourselves and probably wearing a whole series of masks. When people fail, truth means that we must talk to them about what they've done – we can't just sweep it under the carpet. But grace means that our aim is always to restore people, to bring them back to the place where they were before they messed up.

I WISH I'D WRITTEN THIS

Dick Staub in his book The Culturally Savvy Christian writes 'We tend to err on the side of grace or truth. We either love people unconditionally, not delivering the truth about their need to change, or we deliver the truth without showing them unconditional love. Jesus' approach can be summarised as follows. Truth without grace is legalism. Grace without truth is romanticism. Truth with grace is dynamism. Jesus demonstrated that loving a person does not require us to abandon the truth, nor does truth demand that we neglect love. Jesus was full of both grace and truth, and when Jesus is at work within us, our lives will display the same exquisite fullness.' [26]

A peach community is fundamentally a community which is full of grace and truth expressed to those outside the community, and grace and truth expressed to those within. Let's aim for that same 'exquisite fullness' in our church and in our lives.

What's So Amazing About Grace?
Philip Yancey

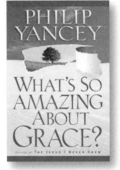

If there's one book I would encourage everyone in our community to read at least once in their life (other than the Bible of course) it would be this one. It transformed my understanding of grace, what it means and what a beautiful concept it is when worked out in practice.

The Culturally Savvy Christian
Dick Staub

A fascinating book on how we should engage with popular culture in a way which combines both grace and truth.

SUGGESTED RESOURCES

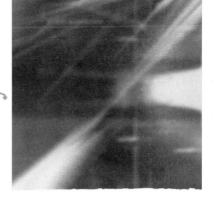

messy

...everything should
be done in a
fitting and orderly way.

(1 Corinthians 14:40)

I went to a leadership event a few years ago, where someone spoke about getting and implementing a vision for the life of a church. The speaker laid out a simple plan. All you needed to do was go home, gather a group together to get a vision from God, come up with a strategy to make that vision a reality and then announce it to the rest of the church – job done! How could that possibly take more than a couple of weeks, perhaps a month at most? It sounded so simple.

This was just around the time I was taking over leading the church, and as I reflected on what had been said I asked an older and wiser leader what he thought about the talk. His response was that what the leader had just described would probably take at least five years to work through and turn into a reality.

I realise that there could be a similar danger with what I'm describing here. That it can make everything sound very tidy, simple and straightforward. That in this peachy church we've been talking about, all we'll have are amazing stories of changed lives, restored marriages, addicts who are now free of their addictions, people who have found a hope and a purpose in their lives, and that every Sunday it will be filled with happy smiling people with totally sorted lives. If only!

Of course the reality is very different. Building a genuinely peachy church will produce what can feel at times like chaos. All sorts of broken people coming into the community, being honest and open about their issues making a mess all over the place. Leadership challenges, diversity challenges, doctrinal issues being raised, people messing up. Yet in the midst of it all God is at work changing lives (sounds a lot like the book of Acts).

Erwin McManus, leader of Mosaic Church in Los Angeles, reminds us that the most orderly community on earth is a graveyard. Everyone is exactly where they are supposed to be, doing exactly what they are supposed to be doing. Perfect order! But that isn't what God has in mind when he talks about everything being done in order. He wants much more the order of the maternity ward. All around is screaming, sick, poo and chaos, yet there is a sense of order, and instead of death there is an incredible sense of new life breaking out everywhere.

So let's be prepared for the mess. In this belong ▶ believe ▶ behave community there will be people who even when they've believed take a long time genuinely to get to the behaving bit. Remember that three years after Jesus started working on the disciples they were still falling asleep when he'd asked them to pray for him, cutting off ears which he had to put back again and denying him when they'd promised to stay with him to the end. Even the disciples, with the input of Jesus, were still a messy work in progress – how much more is that going to be true of us?

SO WHAT MIGHT THE MESS LOOK LIKE?

Some of the mess will be people beginning to sort out broken lives in the new reality of their relationship with God. Things which have remained hidden for years coming into the light. Past hurts, failures and addictions being brought into the open. Broken relationships being put back together again. Wrestling with the lifestyle changes which God requires. People expressing their doubts and asking questions to which there are no easy answers.

Similarly, as we begin to help other people deal with their pasts, unresolved issues in our own past can surface and cause us pain. We can so easily think that we've got our own lives all sorted and dealt with, only for something somebody else is going through to open up old wounds.

Some of the mess will result in those of us at the core of the church community having our own attitudes exposed as new people come to us with their mess. Nothing reveals our own hearts, our own selfishness, our own pride, our own judgementalism and our own lack of love more quickly than trying to love another human being who is going through a tough time. There is a lot of truth in the saying 'hurting people hurt people', and we need truly to learn what it means to 'love your neighbour as yourself'.

Some of the mess will be things being disclosed which require us to work with the police, social services and other statutory agencies. Sometimes people will want to join our community who have a 'past' which means they may pose a risk to the young and the vulnerable. Sometimes we will hear of abuse or other alleged incidents where we have to decide how much we need to disclose to social services and the police, both to comply with the law and to protect ourselves.

Some of the mess will be leaders having to seek God for genuine spiritual guidance, as being peachy means we can't just have a rule book telling us what to do in any given situation.

Some of the mess will be trying to change culture, and people struggling or just refusing to do things in new ways.

Some of the mess will be the pain of people leaving us as they can't cope with the level of mess.

Some of the mess will be the pain of watching people who have started well falling away.

It will be messy. But Proverbs 14:4 reminds us that 'Where there are no oxen, the manger is clean, but abundant crops come by the strength of the ox.' (ESV)

If we want to see an abundant harvest, it isn't going to come without some mess. So let's be prepared for it, let's not be surprised by it, and let's rejoice that although the manger might be messy we are creating the right environment for an abundant crop.

....

The Barbarian Way
Erwin McManus
Erwin gives a radical call away from 'civilised' Christianity towards something which is untamed and far more raw. The faith he

SUGGESTED RESOURCES

describes is definitely messy! If you get a chance please watch the DVD of Erwin preaching the message of this book at the Willow Creek Leadership Summit in 2003.

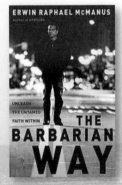

unmasked

In a Greek drama when an actor wanted to play a character they would pretend to be that person by putting on a mask. In fact in Greek the words for 'actor' and 'hypocrite' are the same, meaning to put on a mask.

One of the things that happens in a coconut community is that you get a lot of mask wearing. In order to belong you need at least to pretend to be behaving, so people feel a strong need to put on masks, rather than be real about what is going on in their lives and their worlds. We see this in Jesus' analysis of the lives of the Pharisees in the verse above, that what was on the outside didn't match what was on the inside.

We want to encourage and foster the exact opposite. To create an environment and a culture where people can take off their masks, and be honest and open about their struggles.

This doesn't go just for new people joining our community, but for everyone who is part of the church. Vulnerability breeds vulnerability, and once those of us who have been around for years are able to take off our masks and be real about who we are, newcomers will feel similarly able to be vulnerable.

There are a number of areas of our lives where we can end up wearing masks to try and cover up what is there.

PAST HURTS

I used frequently to make the mistake of judging people by what I saw on the outside. I'd meet happy, smiling people and assume that they'd had idyllic childhoods and nothing sad or bad had ever happened to them. Leading the church has taught me that just isn't true, and I'm no longer shocked by anything that anyone tells me.

We all carry with us a bunch of hurts from the past. We need to get those hurts out in the open and deal with them, in order that we don't allow our past to define our future. Often that will involve forgiving the people who have hurt us.

Past hurts may have come from parents, teachers, siblings, partners, church leaders, neighbours, friends, even from people we've never even met but whose words or actions have affected us in some way.

Our peach community should be a safe place where we can deal with our past hurts, confident in the knowledge that we're not going to be condemned or rejected but helped to find healing and restoration. Many people work past hurts out in one-on-one conversations or in a small group. For others it might take a structured course such as our bereavement course or Freedom in Christ. Others may need professional counselling.

Whatever it takes for you, please have the courage to take off the mask of past hurts and let people see the real you.

PAST FAILURES

We are all messed up, broken people who have not only been hurt, but have made mistakes which have hurt and let down other people, and sinned against God.

Some people struggle ever to forgive themselves for what they have done, particularly if they have to deal with the results of their failure every day. Others struggle to find a place where they can be forgiven, a community which will accept them without constantly seeing them through the lens of their failure.

I often talk about us being a church of the second chance. Too often I've seen Christians who have messed up being told they are no longer of any use to God. Yes, there will be consequences for our sin, but the church must be a place of forgiveness, reconciliation and restoration.

DOUBTS

In a coconut community people can be afraid to express doubts, since in order to belong you need first to be seen to be solid about what you believe. We need to create a community where it is safe for everyone, even long-time followers of Christ, to express and explore their doubts. Timothy Keller in his book The Reason for God puts it like this:

A faith without some doubts is like a human body without any antibodies in it. People who blithely go through life too busy or indifferent to ask hard questions about why they believe as they do will find themselves defenceless against either the experience of tragedy or the probing questions of a smart sceptic. A person's faith can collapse almost overnight if she has failed over the years to listen patiently to her own doubts, which should only be discarded after long reflection ...[27]

Only if you struggle long and hard with objections to your faith will you be able to provide grounds for your beliefs to sceptics, including yourself, that are plausible rather than ridiculous or offensive.

All of us must feel able to express our doubts and fears, to discuss them and to explore the answers to the questions we may have.

STRUGGLES

We all have areas of life we struggle with, areas where we are weak or which through the circumstances of life are just hard work. For some it might be an addiction, for others it might be fears, anger, illness, unemployment, financial difficulties, relationship difficulties, singleness, bringing up children as a single parent, all manner of different issues.

We can often feel ashamed of the areas we struggle with, yet we need to learn to be open and honest about them.

Some of us will need practical support, which we must never be too proud to accept. I remember a time when Catrina and I had virtually no money. When our car broke down some friends gave us some money towards buying a new one, which both humbled us and blessed us immeasurably. Some of us will need emotional support. Addicts may need a group of people they can regularly meet with and be accountable to. And some of us will need spiritual support, people who will stand with us in prayer, lending us their faith when we feel like ours isn't enough.

Whatever it is, we need to be a community which doesn't run away from struggling people as though they had some form of leprosy, but moves towards them and offers whatever support we are able to. And when we are struggling, which we will all do from time to time, we need to be open and humble enough to ask for help and accept the help we receive.

SUFFERING

Some Christians have a theology which says that as a follower of Christ your life should be one of health, wealth and everything going up and to the right. Yet I've seen Christians who've been generous with their money all their lives get into financial difficulty through business failures which were none of their fault, Christians who have exercised and eaten healthily all their lives get cancer, and Christians who love God with a passion lose loved ones and go through indescribable pain.

Jesus told us that in this world we would have trouble,[28] he wept at the tomb of Lazarus; [29] Paul wrote about what it was to know financial hardship and hunger[30] and he wrote to Timothy about how to medicate his stomach complaint. [31]

When we're the ones going through trouble we need to be open and honest about what is happening in our world, particularly if it is an ongoing situation which isn't going to be resolved in a few days or weeks.

PLEASING OTHERS

Another mask which I strongly believe many of us wear (at least one I'm regularly tempted to wear) is created in response to the pressure to please others, to behave in the way either that they want me to behave or that I feel I need to behave in order to have them as my friends.

This can manifest itself in many ways. The woman who feels that she needs to dress a certain way or have a certain body shape to be considered beautiful. The man who feels he is defined by the job he does, the car he drives or the house he lives in. The mum who feels she needs to join in with the gossip at the school gate in order to be 'in'. The teenager who feels the pressure to smoke or get drunk 'because that's what all my friends are doing'. The leader who makes decisions based on how popular or unpopular they are going to be. We need to learn to be people who are defined not by what others think of us but by what God thinks of us, and to be willing to be who God created us to be in each and every situation we walk into.

FEAR OF REJOICING

A final mask which I think we can end up wearing is in some ways the opposite of the ones I've described so far. That is a fear of rejoicing when things go well. We can become so aware of, and sensitive to, what is going on in the people around us that we feel uncomfortable about talking about good things that happen to us. Paul told us that we should 'Rejoice with those who rejoice; mourn with those who mourn'.[32]

So, yes, we are sensitive to people who may be struggling, but not to such an extent that we don't talk about all the great things God is doing in our lives and our community. So we rejoice extravagantly with the couple who have just heard they are going to have a baby, even when there are other couples longing to have a child. We get so excited when a couple get married, even when there are single people in our community still searching for a partner. We're delighted for the person who has just got a new job, even though there are people who are unemployed in our midst.

Rejoicing is to be a hallmark of our community, and we must resist any pressure to wear a mask that would stop us from declaring when God does good things in our lives.

IN CLOSING

Before we finish this chapter let me ask what masks you feel you need to take off. Are they past hurts, past failures, doubts, struggles, suffering, pleasing others or not rejoicing? If you're aware of one, please stop right now and ask God to give you the courage to take it off, and speak about your mask to somebody you trust.

SUGGESTED RESOURCES

God on Mute
Pete Greig
One of the most honest and open books I have ever read on suffering, and being open and honest with God about our doubts and fears.

The Reason for God
Timothy Keller
Can you have faith without saying goodbye to your brain? This book takes the most common questions about and objections to the Christian faith and answers them in a straightforward but credible way.

NATASHA

natasha

Natasha (not her real name) was born in Wales to parents who emigrated from the West Indies. Family break-ups, bereavement and relationship breakdowns took her to the edge of faith. I was in a family of five children, second eldest to my sister Michelle, with an outwardly solid Christian background – my father was a senior church leader and I taught at Sunday school. Michelle and I were best friends and we did everything together, including prison ministry – teaching inmates about the Christian faith and encouraging them. But in 2001 my parents split up, which came as a huge shock to everyone. A few months later Michelle became very ill with breast cancer. She was hospitalised and given only two weeks to live. I was devastated and prayed with her for healing.

But in September 2002, Michelle passed away and my world fell apart. I couldn't see myself living without her. At this time of utter despair there was no support for me in the places you would usually expect to find it, including in my marriage where I was mentally and emotionally abused. For the first time I asked: 'Who is God and why has he allowed this to happen to our family?' I'd wholeheartedly believed Michelle would be healed and it had never happened.

I was stripped of all the things in life I understood. For the first time ever I cried out to God from my heart: 'Help me – I'm in a deep, dark pit and I'm going to stay here until you pull me out.' Sometimes I read Psalms which reflected the deep hurt I felt and also spoke of God's grace and peace. But he felt so far away.

Slowly and gently God pulled me up. I hurt a little less, but still wasn't really living. I did what I needed to do, such as going to work, but in numbness. Then a couple of years later my husband and I finally split up. At that time I felt God wanted me to go back into prison ministry, but how could I without my sister? I wanted to obey, so said, 'I will serve you, God, but I will not worship you.'

Over the next three years God began to gradually mend my broken heart, but I still had down days. In the run up to Christmas 2007 I felt particularly low and asked God to send one little sign that he cared about my life. The next moment I got a text message from a guy I'd met at a party a few days before, inviting me for a drink. That guy was Mark and now he's my husband! Mark was already part of the Kerith church so I moved to make a new home in Bracknell. For me, serving with him on the Alpha course and then starting a Lifegroup together helped me to take the risk of building new friendships again and to begin trusting others. Now Mark and I also work in prison ministry together.

God taught me what a relationship with him is really about. I learnt that worship is not just about singing songs, but worship is a lifestyle in all situations. Even though we are Christians bad things can still happen, yet when life is at its worst God still works. Things may not turn out how we want them to, but God sees the bigger picture and sometimes has another plan. And now I love God more than I did before.

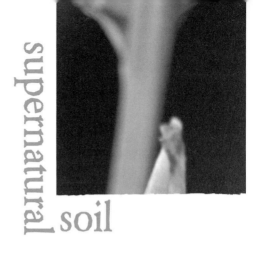

supernatural soil

I planted the seed, Apollos watered it,
but God has been making it grow. So neither
the one who plants nor the one who waters is anything,
but only God, who makes things grow.

(1 Corinthians 3:6–7)

As a child I was always fascinated by bonsai trees. You know the ones, where you take an acorn and put it in a tiny pot, so what could have been a majestic towering oak tree still becomes a perfectly formed oak tree, but only grows to a few inches high.

As a peach community we need to realise that we can't produce growth. As Paul reminds us in his letter to the church in Corinth, God is the only one who makes things grow. But just as with the bonsai, so the environment we create – the soil and the pot we put the seed into – will be a defining factor in how much growth there will be.

One of Jesus' most famous parables is the parable of the sower.[33] In this Jesus talks about seed which falls on a variety of different types of ground. Some falls on a path and is eaten by birds. Some falls on rocky ground where it grows for a while but then dies from lack of roots. Some falls amongst weeds which choke it and stunt its growth. Still other seed falls on good soil where there is an incredible harvest, thirty, sixty or even one hundred times what was sown.

I've often heard this parable used to explain how different people respond to hearing the good news about Jesus, which is certainly valid. We've all known people who responded enthusiastically to the gospel, but then fell away, leaving us wondering what we did wrong. This parable helps us realise that we don't need to be surprised when they don't respond the way we expected.

But this parable is also an encouragement to us to realise that we can affect the soil of our lives and our community. That we can help to create the environment where this incredible life change can take place.

Much of this book deals with the characteristics of the soil which God is calling us to produce. Soil soaked in prayer, soil full of the Holy Spirit, the soil of excellence and much more. But I want to think for a moment on what can happen if we get the soil right.

SUPERNATURAL MULTIPLICATION

Our awareness of the supernatural power of God needs to permeate everything we do. We can plan meetings, courses, small groups. We can come up with strategies, get in outside speakers, run conferences, do all manner of different things. But unless God is in it all then we're wasting our time. As Solomon says in Psalm 127, 'Unless the LORD builds the house, the builders labour in vain.'[34]

All we can ever do is create the environment where God can change lives. But if we can create the right soil then the most amazing things can happen. As we've already seen, the promise of Jesus in the parable of the sower is:

 Still other seed fell on good soil. It came up, grew and produced a crop, some multiplying thirty, some sixty, some a hundred times. (Mark 4:8)

I believe that God is asking us to believe for the most incredible fruitfulness.

Imagine in your own life if God produced a multiplication of what he has sown in you, for your life to result in thirty, sixty or a hundred other lives being changed. God can do that through you, whoever you are and however long you've known God. Remember it doesn't depend on you – it depends on God.

Imagine that happening in the life of our church. Imagine us producing a harvest of what God has sown in us. Imagine our one church developing into thirty, sixty or a hundred churches. That might sound outrageous, but God wants us to believe that the most outrageous things can happen. Imagine the 600 people who were in the church when I took over leading from Ben Davies in 2007 multiplying into 18,000, 36,000 or 60,000. Again that sounds crazy, but that is the fruitfulness Jesus speaks of and wants us to believe can happen. And it's a fruitfulness which is not about us being glorified but about the name of Jesus being exalted.

God wants us to believe him for supernatural fruitfulness.

SUPERNATURAL POWER

God also wants us to believe him for supernatural power. Paul said of his own ministry:

My message and my preaching were not with wise and persuasive words, but with a demonstration of the Spirit's power, so that your faith might not rest on human wisdom, but on God's power. (1 Corinthians 2:4–5)

Central to Paul's message was that he saw the supernatural power of God at work. It can be very tempting in a 'peachy' or 'seeker sensitive' environment to script out the supernatural power of God, and to think that relevant preaching and heartfelt appeals will be enough. We want to push in the opposite direction, doing church in a way that doesn't alienate lost people, but also believing that one of the reasons Jesus ascended into heaven after the resurrection was that the Holy Spirit might come to give us power to be his witnesses. As Jesus said before he ascended into heaven:

But you will receive power when the Holy Spirit comes on you; and you will be my witnesses in Jerusalem, and in all Judea and Samaria, and to the ends of the earth. (Acts 1:8)

On that first day when the Holy Spirit was poured out they saw their first outrageous multiplication. Those initial 120 believers became 3,000 in a single day, a 25-time multiplication in the space of a few hours. And we see it again and again in the book of Acts (which really should be called 'The Acts of the Holy Spirit' rather than its more common title 'The Acts of the Apostles'). Whether it is the crippled beggar being healed,[35] the Holy Spirit being poured out in the house of Cornelius,[36] Paul surviving being bitten by a poisonous snake[37] or all the sick people on the island of Malta being healed,[38] each time the demonstrations of the Spirit's power result in another burst of expansion and growth for the church.

So we will pray for the sick to be healed, believing that God still heals today. We ask God for prophecy and words of knowledge which will bring clarity, direction and hope to people's lives and their situations. But we will do all this in a way which is consistent with our peachy values.

We will also acknowledge that not everyone is healed, and wrestle with what it means to live between the first and second coming of Jesus. We don't yet see all of God's kingdom at work in our lives, but we keep praying, as Jesus taught us to, 'your kingdom come, your will be done, on earth as it is in heaven'. [39]

THE GREATEST MIRACLE

Amidst all this talk of the supernatural I want to make one final observation, which is this. The greatest miracles we will ever see are not incredible healings or miraculous turns of events, but lives changed by the supernatural power of God. Medical science can increasingly do things which even a decade or two ago would have looked like a miracle, but only the power of God can change and transform a human heart. We need to recognise and celebrate that as the greatest miracle we will ever see, both in our own lives and in the lives of others.

I've read of and been to places where it was proclaimed that the supernatural power of God was amazingly at work, with people falling over, being healed and all manner of things going on, and yet there seemed to be little genuine life change. I've been to other places where there was none of that, but lives were quietly being changed left, right and centre.

Yes, let's pray for and expect the most amazing healings, prophecies and miracles. But let's get most excited about people's eternal destinies being changed. I'm reminded of what Jesus said to the seventy-two, when they came back from an outreach trip having seen the most amazing healings and deliverance:

The seventy-two returned with joy and said, 'Lord, even the demons submit to us in your name.' He replied, 'I saw Satan fall like lightning from heaven. I have given you authority to trample on snakes and scorpions and to overcome all the power of the enemy; nothing will harm you. However, do not rejoice that the spirits submit to you, but rejoice that your names are written in heaven.' (Luke 10:17–20)

SUGGESTED RESOURCES

In a Pit with a Lion on a Snowy Day
Mark Batterson

This book, as well as having a crazy title, will challenge you with some of the things you can do personally to create the right environment in your life for growth.

Sun Stand Still
Steven Furtick

If you think you have faith in God, please read this and be deeply challenged about what it truly means to believe God for supernatural growth.

Re-creating the Community of Jesus

treasure

Now the tax collectors and sinners were all
gathering around to hear Jesus.
But the Pharisees and the teachers of the law muttered,
'This man welcomes sinners and eats with them.'
Then Jesus told them this parable:
'Suppose one of you has a hundred sheep and loses one of them.
Doesn't he leave the ninety-nine in the open country and go after
the lost sheep until he finds it?
And when he finds it, he joyfully puts it on his shoulders and goes
home. Then he calls his friends and neighbours together and says,
"Rejoice with me; I have found my lost sheep."
I tell you that in the same way there will be more rejoicing in
heaven over one sinner who repents than over ninety-nine
righteous persons who do not need to repent.'

(Luke 15:1–7)

We've explored the difference between the communities of the peach
and the coconut. Now let's start to look at re-creating the community
of Jesus in practice.

In Luke 15 we read of yet another collision between the
coconut community of the Pharisees and the peachy community of
Jesus, in a way which perfectly highlights the difference between the
two. We read in verse 1:

Now the tax collectors and sinners were all gathering around to hear Jesus.
But the Pharisees and the teachers of the law muttered, 'This man welcomes
sinners and eats with them.'

It's fascinating to me that the Pharisees are gathering around
Jesus, alongside the tax collectors and the sinners. They can't stand
him, but they're fascinated by him and can't just ignore him or stay

away from him. If we were Jesus we might have been tempted just to shrug our shoulders, ignore the Pharisees and get on with talking to the 'sinners', but Jesus demonstrates what true grace looks like. He is as willing to engage with the Pharisees as he is with the rest of the crowd, and in a way designed not to condemn them but to try and lead them into truth.

I love how Jesus engages them. He doesn't take them to Old Testament passages to show them how far they've strayed from God, or thunder out some message of condemnation at their attitude. Instead he tells them three very simple stories about lost things – a lost sheep, a lost coin and finally a lost son – showing how God feels about the tax collectors and sinners they are so quick to write off.

SHEEP

In the first story we read about ninety-nine well behaved sheep who do exactly what they're supposed to, and one badly behaved sheep who wanders off into potential danger. The shepherd leaves behind the ninety-nine 'good' sheep to look for the lost one, and then when he finds it throws a party for all his friends to celebrate. In the same way, Jesus says, God parties more when one lost person turns back to God than over ninety-nine people who have no need to repent. [40]

COINS

In the second story, which seems remarkably similar, a lady has ten coins, but loses one of them. She turns her house upside down looking for it, and again it's party time when she finds it. In the same way, Jesus says, God celebrates when one lost person is found. [41]

SONS

In the third story a father has two sons. The younger son asks for his inheritance early (in their culture effectively saying to the father 'I wish you were dead'). Amazingly the father gives it to him (as the younger brother he'd have got a third of his father's estate). The son then takes off and squanders the money on wine, women and song. Destitute and abandoned by all his alleged friends, he decides to return home, hoping he can at least become a servant in his dad's household. Yet when he returns he finds a father who every day has been looking to the horizon, hoping today might be the day his long-lost son returns. As the son comes towards home, fearing the reception that awaits him, the father runs to him (culturally something a father would never have done) and throws his arms around the son and kisses him. He then has him dressed in the best clothes, and throws a party which he invites all the neighbours to. [42]

OLDER BROTHERS

Often when people tell the story of the 'prodigal son', as this is often known, they finish there, with the father hugging the son and throwing a party. It's a beautiful picture of how God responds to us every time we turn to him. But Jesus hasn't finished yet – he still hasn't got to the point he wants to make to the Pharisees who were criticising him for being a 'friend of sinners'.

In the story the older brother hears news of what has happened, of how the father has greeted the younger son and is throwing a party for him. Yet instead of sharing in the father's joy and welcoming back his long-lost brother he refuses to have anything to do with either of them, revealing the true state of his heart towards both the father and the younger brother.

Jesus is saying to the Pharisees that they are just like the older brother. Jesus has come 'to seek and save the lost', and yet instead of the Pharisees finding delight at the 'sinner' younger brothers who once were lost now being found, they simply refuse to come to the party.

Jesus is also saying that he is our true elder brother. What the elder brother should have done in the story was, on behalf of the father, to go in search of the lost younger brother, and when the lost younger brother was found to share in the party his father was going to throw. That is exactly what Jesus has done, coming from the Father to save all of us lost younger brothers, and then sharing in the Father's delight every time one of us comes back to him.

TREASURE

The message of the three stories is clear. God is passionate about lost people, and deliriously happy every time a lost person comes back to him. He is so passionate about lost people that he sent the most precious thing he had, his only son Jesus, to make it possible for us to return to the Father, and he now expects us to share in the same mission with the same passion and delight he has.

That means that reaching lost people is going to be at the core of everything we do. Our Sunday gatherings, our ministries, our courses, our small group communities and our individual lives are all to be about seeing lost people becoming found people.

In fact it's the whole motivation which lies behind the drive to build a culture which is peachy, which is accessible to people far from

God without ever compromising what is at its core. If we aren't reaching lost people then everything we do is a complete waste of time, and we may as well all give up and go to heaven early.

COMMUNITY IMPLICATIONS

This focus on people being treasure will affect how we do church when there are lost people amongst us. Some of the later chapters deal with this in more detail, but for now I just want us to think for a bit about the style in which we do church. We want to recognise that there aren't any right or wrong styles but just different ones, and ones which may be more or less effective in reaching lost people. Paul expressed this strongly when he wrote:

> Though I am free and belong to no one, I have made myself a slave to everyone, to win as many as possible. To the Jews I became like a Jew, to win the Jews. To those under the law I became like one under the law (though I myself am not under the law), so as to win those under the law. To those not having the law I became like one not having the law (though I am not free from God's law but am under Christ's law), so as to win those not having the law. To the weak I became weak, to win the weak. I have become all things to all people so that by all possible means I might save some. I do all this for the sake of the gospel, that I may share in its blessings. (1 Corinthians 9:19–23)

For Paul the message, the gospel, never changed but the medium, the way he communicated that message, was shaped to the people he was trying to reach.

For us one way this can be expressed is in styles of music. Are hymns better than contemporary songs? No, they're just different. Is worshipping to a rock band less spiritual than worshipping to an organ? No, again they're just different. But which one is most likely to reach lost people in our culture? Probably the rock band doing contemporary songs rather than the organ playing hymns. So that's what we'll do most of the time. Not because it's what I like, or what the leaders or musicians like, but because it's what is most likely to reach lost people.

PERSONAL IMPLICATIONS

The realisation that God is passionate about lost people will also shape our personal lives. Making sure that our lives don't get so busy that all the friends we have are Christians.

Taking every opportunity to share our faith with people we meet. Being the best students, employees and neighbours we can be so that who we are will be attractive to other people.

STAYING PEACHY

I've said already that peaches can quickly turn into coconuts. Peachy communities can quickly become self-absorbed, more interested in those who are in than those who are out, treating people outside as an annoyance rather than the very reason they exist. There are so many 'good' things to be getting on with, meetings to be led, courses to be run, conferences to attend, buildings to be built and issues to be resolved that lost people just get pushed to the edges.

I believe that's as true in our individual lives as it is for the church as a whole. Yet Jesus wants constantly to remind us that the whole reason he came to earth was to 'seek and save the lost', [43] and if we've missed that we've missed everything.

Just Walk Across the Room
Bill Hybels
A book which makes sharing our faith seem something which can be both natural and achievable for every one of us.

SUGGESTED RESOURCES

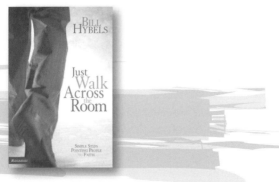

community

All the believers were together and had everything in common. They sold property and possessions to give to anyone who had need. Every day they continued to meet together in the temple courts. They broke bread in their homes and ate together with glad and sincere hearts, praising God and enjoying the favour of all the people. And the Lord added to their number daily those who were being saved.

(Acts 2:44–47)

As we read about Jesus much of his time is spent with large crowds, preaching and ministering to thousands at a time, feeding them, healing them and speaking to their deepest needs and longings. But we read that Jesus also very deliberately gathers a small group of people, the twelve apostles and a small number of people associated with them, who are the people he spends the most of his time with and sows the most of his life into. They are the ones who get to see Jesus up close, to whom he explains the meaning behind some of his parables and who are constantly being taught, corrected, rebuked and above all loved, day after day by him for three years.

We see a similar pattern in the early church. They met in large gatherings in the temple courts – the church had over 3,000 people in it after the day of Pentecost. But they also met in one another's homes, in smaller gatherings, where they could have meals together and build deeper relationships.

Similarly for us our large Sunday meetings are great, but it can be tough to build any depth of relationship. We also need a place other than the Sunday gatherings where we can build deeper friendships, care and pray for one another, grow in our knowledge of God and the Bible and reach out to our friends who are far from God. Bill Hybels describes being in community as 'knowing and being known; loving and being loved; celebrating and being celebrated', [44] something which every one of us deep down longs for.

This desire for community flows from the very nature of God. From the Bible we learn that there is one God, but that he is three persons, the Father, the Son and the Holy Spirit, each of whom is fully God (there is more on this in chapter 26). For all eternity they have lived together in perfect unity, a community where there is no back biting, gossip or jostling for position but just a desire to honour and build one another up. We, created in God's image, are created with that same desire to find genuine long-lasting relationships.

Community is also a necessity if we are to work out Jesus' command to love one another. It is in this community that we are called to care for one another, forgive one another, encourage one another and work out all the other 'one anothers' in the Bible. Sometimes that will be painful, as we rub up against other people and realise how imperfect we are, but it is through doing this that our hearts will be changed. As C.S. Lewis puts it so powerfully: 'To love at all is to be vulnerable. Love anything, and your heart will certainly be wrung and possibly broken. If you want to make sure of keeping it intact, you must give your heart to no one, not even to an animal. Wrap it carefully round with hobbies and little luxuries; avoid all entanglements; lock it up safe in the casket or coffin of your selfishness. But in that casket – safe, dark, motionless, airless – it will change. It will not be broken; it will become unbreakable, impenetrable, irredeemable.' [45]

Our genuine love for one another will also be a powerful witness to the world. Jesus prays 'so that they may be brought to complete unity. Then the world will know that you sent me and have loved them even as you have loved me.' [46]

HOW DO WE WORK THAT OUT IN PRACTICE?

For years we had an expectation that everybody who was part of our church would be part of an organised small group, which in those days were called housegroups (for some of those years you could only go to a housegroup for two weeks if you weren't a member – we weren't so peachy in those days!). These groups would usually meet midweek in a home, and the meeting would be made up of what we called the four W's: welcome, worship, word and witness. Much of that model was adopted from churches in Asia, many of which operate along what is called a 'cell church' model, where everybody is committed to being part of a very structured, ordered group similar to the one I've described.

My observation is that the attempts by western churches to adopt the cell church model have by and large been a failure. The promise was that if churches 'transitioned to cell' they would see explosive growth both numerically and in depth of spirituality. The reality is that just hasn't happened. We made the mistake of confusing a biblical principle (the importance of building deep meaningful relationships with a small number of people) with a methodology which worked in a particular cultural context but not in ours.

If I'm honest I haven't seen a church in the UK, or in fact anywhere in the western world, which has truly cracked small groups in a structured way which works for everyone. As a pastor I'd love to get a report every week which tells me what percentage of our community attended a small group last week, with a spreadsheet to say who went to which one. But I don't believe that is ever going to happen, or that it should even be an aspiration for us.

SO WHAT ARE WE GOING TO DO?

First of all we'll uphold the importance of everyone building deep, lasting relationships with a small group of people. People who are going to care for you when tough times come, people who will cry with you, laugh with you and do life with you, and for whom you can do the same. I've just heard of a guy in our community who was made redundant yesterday, and that last night two of his friends went round to see him to encourage him and pray for him. We all need those sorts of friendships.

But what we've learnt is that there isn't one structure which is going to work for everyone. Some people will find their own group of friends without any help from the church. I know some of the Africans in our church who just raise their eyebrows at me when I talk to them about being in a small group organised by the church. Community is such a high value in their culture that they're constantly in and out of one another's homes without anyone needing to organise a night of the week for them to meet up.

But others are looking for a structured place to meet up, and to help them to start to build friendships within the church. We realise that these small groups will take a number of different forms, but there are certain things we'll expect to see in each of them. We'd expect each of them to be outward-looking, to include time to care for one another and to have a God part to what goes on. That means that a bunch of guys meeting solely to play squash doesn't qualify, but if every other time they meet they have a Bible study and pray for one another then that could be a small group. We also expect our small groups to display all the peach characteristics we've already talked about. They must be open to all sorts of people joining them, must embrace diversity and must always be fighting the temptation to be inward-looking or cliquey.

There are three different expressions of centrally organised small groups which I'll touch on briefly.

LIFEGROUPS

Many people will find their small group community in a Lifegroup. They meet at an increasingly varied number of times and places, usually in people's homes. Central to most of them would be time to build relationships with one another, study the message from the previous Sunday, worship together and reach out to unbelieving friends and relatives. You can find details of all the Lifegroups on our church website, www.kerith.co.uk, and on a Sunday the welcome team will be able to help you with finding one. We'd encourage people to try several in order to find one that works well for them.

Lifegroups often have a life of their own, with new groups being started and other groups coming to a natural end all the time, so please don't expect to be in the same group for ever!

We also encourage the idea of people starting Lifegroups. If you'd like to think about starting one then please contact the leaders of our Lifegroup ministry (see the website) and we can look at getting you on our Lifegroup Academy so that you can lead a group.

SERVING GROUPS

Some serving areas in church also act as small group communities. This won't be true of all serving areas, as in many there isn't time to do anything other than the job at hand, but others such as our musicians or the Foodbank team can provide that dual function.

COURSES

For others their initial small group community will be found in a course. Obviously this isn't going to last for ever, although we do have courses which last for up to two years. Many people find a course a great starting point for small group life.

You can find a full list of courses currently running on the website, or in the latest LinK magazine.

OTHER EXPRESSIONS

We are very open to other people finding their own expression of small group community. For instance we have groups of tradespeople meeting for breakfast to support and pray for one another, and groups of mums meeting to pray and study the Bible together. None of these have any direct church oversight, although we do expect an openness to leadership input and direction, and a level of accountability as to what is going on in the group. As long as those are in place we're really open to people finding their own ways to express community.

A GROUP FOR EVERYONE

Over the coming years we believe God will send large numbers of new people to join us. We want to be a church where every new person who comes to us can find a small group community which works for them. A group that meets at a convenient time and place, where they feel at home and where they can grow in their relationships with God and with the friends they make in that group.

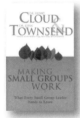

Making Small Groups Work
Dr Henry Cloud and
Dr John Townsend
A great resource for anyone looking to lead a small group.

Kerith Website (www.kerith.co.uk)
Here you'll find a list of all our Lifegroups, courses and serving communities.

Pastoral Team
Our pastoral team exist to help people integrate into the life of the church. If you're struggling to get into a group then please speak to them, either on a Sunday or via the website, and they'll do everything they can to help you find a group which will work for you.

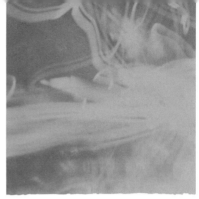

conflict

If your brother or sister sins, go and point out their fault, just
between the two of you.
If they listen to you, you have won them over.
But if they will not listen, take one or two others along,
so that 'every matter may be established by the testimony of two
or three witnesses.' If they still refuse to listen,
tell it to the church; and if they refuse to listen even to the
church, treat them as you would a pagan or a tax collector.

(Matthew 18:15–17)

It would be nice to think that in our peachy community there would
be no conflict. That people would never fall out, disagree, hurt one
another and even leave the church because there's somebody they
can't get on with – dream on!

Sadly conflict is inevitable in human relationships. When sin
first entered the world, one of the results was a breakdown in the
relationship between Adam and Eve. They descended into the first
husband and wife fall-out when God asked Adam whether he'd eaten
from the tree and Adam responded, 'The woman you put here with
me—she gave me some fruit from the tree, and I ate it.' [47] Not much
later we find Cain murdering Abel. And things aren't much different
when we get to the New Testament. Paul and Barnabas fall out:

> Some time later Paul said to Barnabas, 'Let us go back and visit the believers in
> all the towns where we preached the word of the Lord and see how they are
> doing.' Barnabas wanted to take John, also called Mark, with them, but Paul did
> not think it wise to take him, because he had deserted them in Pamphylia and had
> not continued with them in the work. They had such a sharp disagreement that
> they parted company. (Acts 15:36–39)

Later, Paul has to write to the church in Philippi encouraging two women to fix a broken relationship:

> I plead with Euodia and I plead with Syntyche to be of the same mind in the Lord. Yes, and I ask you, my true companion, help these women since they have contended at my side in the cause of the gospel, along with Clement and the rest of my co-workers, whose names are in the book of life. (Philippians 4:2–3)

Not only is conflict inevitable, but most of us don't handle conflict well when it comes. We teach on the marriage course that when we fall out some of us (like me) respond like hedgehogs and withdraw into ourselves and go all quiet, whereas others respond like rhinos and go on the warpath. Neither approach is right or helpful in resolving conflict. The Bible is clear that anger in and of itself isn't wrong – in fact it is often an indication, like a warning light, that there is an issue which needs to be resolved. Jesus seemed to get pretty angry when he drove the money changers out of the temple,[48] but it was a righteous anger against something which was wrong. The important thing is 'in your anger do not sin'. [49] It's not about what you feel but how you deal with it.

We might have a hope that in authentic peachy communities there might be less conflict, but that doesn't seem to be the case – in fact the opposite often seems to be true. In coconut communities where people are wearing masks and not displaying who they really are, and where people who are broken and messed up aren't allowed in, conflict can get avoided and buried. But as we begin to take off the masks and reveal who we really are, and as we start to allow people into our community who are different from us and don't yet know how to behave, conflict becomes more and more likely.

So we mustn't be surprised when conflict comes. But we must make sure that when it does come we deal with it in a godly and mature way. In fact I believe this can be one of the greatest measures of Christian maturity. I've seen far too many allegedly mature believers who when faced with a relationship breakdown have run away from it rather than attempt to resolve it.

So how do we begin to resolve conflict? Well, not surprisingly for such an important subject, the Bible is incredibly clear on how we should go about doing it.

DON'T GOSSIP
Step one for conflict resolution is not to talk to anyone other than

God and the person you are in conflict with. The Bible calls talking to someone else gossip, however much we might like to couch it in language such as 'I'm just telling you so you can pray'. I love what Rick Warren has to say on this:

> When offended by others tell God, not gossipers. Take it to the Throne, not the phone! God reduces hurt. Gossip reinforces it.

Gossip just makes things worse. Many times I've been in situations where I've gossiped about an offence, and then long after I've resolved the conflict the person I've gossiped to still has a problem with the person who offended me. In particular we need to be careful in our age of social media. Facebook, Twitter, BlackBerry Messenger (BBM) and blogs open up a whole new world of ways to spread gossip.

When you're offended, pray, and resist the temptation to talk to anyone other than the person you've fallen out with.

CAN YOU OVERLOOK THE OFFENCE?

The first question to ask when somebody offends you, or seems offended by something you've done, is 'can I simply overlook this?' Proverbs 19:11 teaches us that:

> A person's wisdom yields patience;
> it is to one's glory to overlook an offence.

One of the things I've learnt in ministry is that 'hurting people hurt people'. Many times in the past (and I'm sure it will happen again in the future) somebody has reacted to something I've done in a way which seems totally out of proportion. Usually I've discovered later down the line that there was some other issue going on in that person's life which caused them to react in the way they did. Actually the issue wasn't me but something else going on. Trying to deal with the offence in such a situation is just going to make things worse, as you aren't dealing with the root of the problem. Instead begin to ask God how you can help be part of the process of healing in this person's life.

WHAT IF YOU CAN'T OVERLOOK THE OFFENCE?

If overlooking the offence doesn't work, if it doesn't restore peace in your heart, then Jesus gives us a step-by-step model of how to resolve conflict if we feel we do need to confront the other person.

Let's work our way through what he has to say.

First he says we need to go directly to the person we have the issue with. We've already talked about not gossiping, but let me say again how much heartache and hassle could be avoided if we followed this simple rule. The social networking phenomenon is another place where not to work all this out. I see more and more cases where an offended person will first 'unfriend' the other person on Facebook (if they were friends in the first place) and then use their status to inform all and sundry of what has happened. Please can I be clear that this isn't a helpful, mature, biblical or godly way of resolving conflict?

Let me repeat the words of Jesus in Matthew 18:15, just in case they weren't clear enough:

> **If your brother or sister sins, go and point out their fault, just between the two of you.**

Don't talk to anyone else, don't put it out on Facebook, don't tweet about it, don't send an email or text about it to your best friends, just go straight to the other person.

And if you're going to do this, please can I encourage you actually to go physically? Meet up with the person face to face. Don't email them. I find that people get all brave when they send emails, and they will say things they would never say face to face. Often it can be a coward's way out; be courageous and do it face to face. In a similar way don't do it via letter, text, BBM, MSN or even by phone. With all of those forms of communication it's impossible to read facial expressions and body language which form so much of our communication. When Jesus says 'go' he means 'go'.

WHAT IF THAT DOESN'T WORK?

My experience is that face-to-face contact, with a genuine desire to restore the relationship rather than win a war of words, is enough to resolve most conflicts. But if that doesn't work Jesus is very clear about what to do next.

> **But if they will not listen, take one or two others along, so that 'every matter may be established by the testimony of two or three witnesses.' If they still refuse to listen, tell it to the church; and if they refuse to listen even to the church, treat them as you would a pagan or a tax collector. (Matthew 18:16–17)**

There is an escalation process here. At this stage including other people is not gossip, but the next step in trying to deal with the issue.

My advice would be to find a trusted third party, who knows both of you but is impartial and wise enough not to take sides, and ask them to try and help you resolve the issue. Sit down with the third person as a mediator, to help you process how both of you feel. Then if that doesn't work it needs to be taken to yet another level, ending up with the elders if it needs to go that far.

CONCLUSION

Conflict is inevitable, and if you are part of our church community then there will come a time when you fall out with someone in our community, or someone else falls out with you. Please don't be surprised when it happens, or suddenly feel that the church isn't really all that it was made out to be. It's part of life, and the question is not whether or not it happens, but how mature we are in dealing with it.

The Peacemaker
Ken Sande
Concentrated, practical, biblical wisdom on how to resolve conflict. If you're in a conflict situation which seems unresolvable then please get a copy of this book and put Ken Sande's biblical wisdom into practice.

SUGGESTED RESOURCES

Everybody's Normal Till You Get to Know Them
John Ortberg
This is the best and most practical book I've ever read on the subject of understanding and prospering in our relationships with one another.

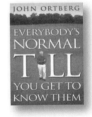

Men are from Mars, Women are from Venus
John Gray
My observation is that lots of conflict within marriage is due to the failure to understand the different ways God has wired men and women. I'd recommend this both to married couples and to singles as they seek to understand why the opposite sex can often seem to be such a mystery.

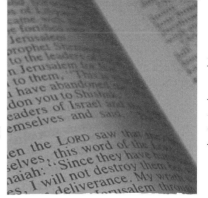

scripture

> **Now the Berean Jews were of more noble character than those in Thessalonica, for they received the message with great eagerness and examined the Scriptures every day to see if what Paul said was true.**

(Acts 17:11)

Hopefully by now you've picked up that the Bible is the source of all that we are talking about in this book, and just as the Berean Jews did I'd encourage you to examine the Bible, the scriptures, to see if all that I'm saying is true! So why is the Bible so important to us? Paul wrote to his young protégé Timothy that:

> All Scripture is God-breathed and is useful for teaching, rebuking, correcting and training in righteousness, so that the servant of God may be thoroughly equipped for every good work. (2 Timothy 3:16–17)

We believe that the Bible, although written by human beings, was inspired and authored by God, and that both the Old and New Testament are the written Word of God. They are our final authority for both what we are to believe about God and how we are to live our lives.

COCONUTS AND THE BIBLE

However, we also recognise that having the Bible in and of itself is not enough. It is incredibly sobering to realise that the Pharisees, the very people who rejected Jesus and ultimately had him crucified, were the people in their community who knew the Bible the best and were the most committed to trying to live according to what it said. Jesus summarised this when he said:

> You study the Scriptures diligently because you think that in them you have eternal life. These are the very Scriptures that testify about me, yet you refuse to come to me to have life. (John 5:39–40)

You can be full of the Bible, and full of knowledge and information about the Bible, but also be at the centre of a coconut community and totally miss what God is doing right under your nose. That should be a huge wake up call to all of us.

PEACHY BIBLE

So how do we avoid making the same mistake as the Pharisees?

Well, we don't go to the opposite extreme, throw the Bible out and just live off our feelings, what seems right or a string of prophetic words. The Bible should be our final authority in everything with regard to who God is, how we relate to him and how he wants us to live, and we need to hold it in the highest regard.

But we do need to understand the purpose of the Bible, that it is not an end in itself but is there to point us to God and to help us to live out the life he has called us to. That means that our aim every time we interact with the Bible is not just to get knowledge or information about the Bible into us, and just become experts on the Bible itself, but instead to see our lives changed as we understand the truths of the Bible, interact with them and apply them to our lives.

That impacts how we preach on a Sunday. Not preaching just to get the Bible into people, but preaching so that our lives will be changed as we embrace and apply biblical truth. It also impacts what we do outside Sundays, providing different environments where everyone, from somebody who isn't yet a Christian to somebody who has been to Bible college and can read the Bible in the original Greek and Hebrew, can get help to understand and apply the Bible at a deeper level. That means everything from the Alpha course at one end to InVest, our two-year course to study the Bible at a deeper level, at the other.

SELF FEEDERS

We also want to place an incredibly high value on teaching people to read and apply the Bible for themselves.

Some Christians seem to have this weird idea that they come to church on a Sunday to be spiritually fed, and then they need to try to survive for the whole week until they can get fed again the following Sunday. To me that seems like madness. As our children were growing up Catrina and I taught them to feed themselves. No longer did we have to play 'aeroplanes' to try and get food into their mouths; instead they learnt to hold their own knife and fork, and eventually even cook and prepare their own meals. As Christians we are called to do the same. Yes, hopefully we get fed and inspired on a Sunday, but there is no way we should then be fasting for the rest of the week before we eat again. Instead each of us needs to learn how to feed ourselves.

We encourage everyone to have a personal Bible reading plan, not leaving it to chance or playing Bible roulette and just seeing where it falls open every day. Some are disciplined enough to sort this out on their own. Others use Bible reading notes. For many of us, we use the YouVersion plans, which come with the YouVersion app which you can download for your iPad, iPhone, Android or BlackBerry phone. This gives you a different passage to read each day in a systematic journey through the scriptures. I never cease to be amazed by how often my reading plans take me to exactly the verse I need for a given situation.

TRANSLATIONS

People sometimes ask about the difference between different Bible translations, and whether there is one 'right' or 'proper' translation to use.

The Bible was originally written in Hebrew (the Old Testament) or Greek (the New Testament) with a few bits written in Aramaic. When people come to translate the Bible into English, as when translating anything from one language to another, they have to make a decision about what philosophy of translation they are going to use.

At one end of the spectrum is a 'word for word' translation, where the translators attempt to take each word in the original language and convert it into the equivalent word in English.

That's not always possible, as the word order in the original language may make no sense in English, there may not be an English word to match the Hebrew or Greek word, and extra words may need to be added to make it make sense, but wherever possible the intention is to make the translation as direct as possible. The problem with 'word for word' translations is that the English in them sometimes feels awkward or clumsy because of the desire to be as close as possible to the original. Having the original author's words doesn't necessarily mean you know what they were thinking.

At the other end of the spectrum is a 'thought for thought' translation, where the translator attempts to express the thoughts or ideas the original author was trying to express, rather than just translating the words. This can be helpful as the same words can mean something very different today from what they meant 2,000 or more years ago. Differences in culture mean that we may understand a given event, story or idea very differently from the people who first read it. The obvious problem with a 'thought for thought' translation is that you are at the mercy of how good the translator is at understanding the author's original thoughts. If they've got that wrong then the translation will be wrong, misleading and potentially heretical!

My recommendation is to use a range of translations. If you want to study a passage in depth use a 'word for word' translation such as the English Standard Version (ESV). For everyday use and ease of reading try something which is a mixture of the two styles such as the New International Version (NIV), and for 'something different' which might give you a fresh perspective on a passage take a look at The Message.

All this having been said, as a church we have adopted a 'house' Bible, which is the default Bible which we use on a Sunday and in our courses. Currently this is the 2011 version of the New International Version.

FINAL THOUGHTS

The Bible is incredibly important in shaping who we are, how we understand God and how we relate to him. However, we must never end up worshipping the Bible, or getting so caught up in the Bible that in the process we miss God.

SUGGESTED RESOURCES

How to Read the Bible for All Its Worth
Gordon D. Fee and Douglas Stuart

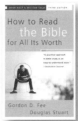

A really good introduction, both to the Bible itself and to how to get the most out of it.

Study Bible:
English Standard Version (ESV)

If you're only going to have one Bible study tool I would recommend the ESV Study Bible. The introductions and commentaries on each book are outstanding, as are the many articles it contains.

YouVersion.com

We live in an age when many people now use Bibles on phones and tablets, rather than carrying around paper Bibles. YouVersion is a great Bible app, which not only gives you pretty much every Bible translation going but also has numerous Bible reading plans. And it's free!

Biblegateway.com

An easy to use website with commentaries on books of the Bible as well as a concordance, where you can look up references to individual words through the Bible.

prayer

> And when you pray, do not be like the hypocrites,
> for they love to pray standing in the
> synagogues and on the street corners to be seen
> by others.
> Truly I tell you, they have received their reward
> in full. But when you pray, go into your room,
> close the door and pray to your Father,
> who is unseen. Then your Father, who sees what
> is done in secret, will reward you. And when you
> pray, do not keep on babbling like pagans,
> for they think they will be heard
> because of their many words. Do not be like them,
> for your Father knows what you need before you ask him.

(Matthew 6:5–8)

We might like to think that prayer would be one of the markers of true spirituality. That the people who pray for hours and hours at a time, or the people who pray long eloquent prayers using language from another century, or the people who pray in prominent places, being seen by many, are the truly spiritual people. Yet one of the messages of Jesus was that it is possible to have a life filled with prayer and totally miss God.

Let's even dare to take that a bit further. This is true not just of individuals but of spiritual communities too. It is possible for a community to have a diary full of prayer meetings and have the whole of their life together peppered with prayer, but for the whole community to miss God. You can be a praying coconut or a praying tomato!

On one occasion Jesus told the story of two people coming to the temple to pray, one a Pharisee and the other a tax collector.

The Pharisee prays:

> God, I thank you that I am not like other people -robbers, evildoers, adulterers -or even like this tax collector. I fast twice a week and give a tenth of all I get. (Luke 18:11–12)

The Pharisee looks very spiritual; he's praying, fasting and tithing, doing all the 'right' things. The tax collector meanwhile prays a very different prayer:

> God, have mercy on me, a sinner. (Luke 18:13)

Far fewer words, far less eloquent, on the surface far less spiritual, and yet he is the one who, according to Jesus, connects with God and has his prayer answered.

We are called to be a community which is characterised by prayer. Jesus said three times in the passage quoted at the start of this chapter 'when you pray', expressing that a key part of following him is cultivating a life of prayer, and he said of his church, quoting the prophet Jeremiah:

> Is it not written: 'My house will be called a house of prayer for all nations'? (Mark 11:17)

And as we read through the book of Acts we realise how prayer was at the centre of everything that happened in the early church, whether it is the disciples waiting for the Holy Spirit to be poured out at Pentecost,[50] one of the hallmarks of the fledgling community,[51] a cripple being healed as Peter is on his way to a prayer meeting,[52] the disciples being filled with the Holy Spirit and boldness when they pray,[53] a key focus for the apostles,[54] what Saul does straight after his conversion,[55] where God speaks to Peter about salvation for the Gentiles[56] or the first response of the church when Peter is thrown into jail.[57] I could go on with many more examples from Acts, but I won't!

Prayer is key to who we are, both as individuals and as a community, and needs to be at the centre of the culture we are building.

So here is the tension for us as a community. How do we make sure it is the prayer Jesus wants us to pray, prayer which genuinely connects us to God? Well, I believe a key to that can be found in Paul's letter to the church in Ephesus, where he writes (talking about Jesus):

> For through him we both have access to the Father by one Spirit. (Ephesians 2:18)

Let's take that apart to see what the prayer we long for looks like.

TO THE FATHER

The power of your prayer depends not on how you pray (standing, kneeling or lying on the ground), what you pray, where you pray, when you pray or for how long you pray, but to whom you pray. If in your praying you connect with God, then all of heaven's resources are available to you. If all you do is speak to the ceiling and impress a few people around you, then, as Jesus said, 'You have received your reward in full'.

Pretty much everyone prays sometimes. Christians, Buddhists, Muslims, Sikhs, even atheists turn to prayer when things get bad enough (as I heard someone say recently, there are no atheists on an aeroplane when it hits turbulence). Prayer on its own doesn't make you spiritual or take you closer to God; what matters is who you are praying to.

Jesus reminds us of this at the very beginning of the Lord's prayer, with the words 'Our Father'. At the heart of prayer is not a ritual or a religious observance but a relationship.

That's a relationship where we understand both who we are, a sinner deserving nothing and in need of mercy, and who he is, the all knowing, all seeing, all powerful timeless creator of the universe who longs to have a loving relationship with messed up sinners like me and you.

It also gives us faith as we pray and ask God for things. If in human terms I need a million pounds, I'm best off asking a millionaire to give it to me, and preferably one who likes me! As children of God we can come to the one who created everything. Jesus states this powerfully when he talks to the disciples about prayer:

> Which of you, if your son asks for bread, will give him a stone? Or if he asks for a fish, will give him a snake? If you, then, though you are evil, know how to give good gifts to your children, how much more will your Father in heaven give good gifts to those who ask him! (Matthew 7:9–11)

Let's not be afraid to ask our heavenly Father for good gifts. But let's also realise that our relationship with God is not based on seeking gifts, even good ones, but seeking him and a relationship with him. And it's not necessarily about us having all our prayers answered, and God just being some sort of celestial slot machine to get us what we want.

Instead when Jesus taught us to pray to the Father he taught us to pray:

> Your kingdom come, your will be done, on earth as it is in heaven. (Matthew 6:10)

Thus when we pray it's not about seeing our will being done, but his. And not about seeing our kingdom come but his. I believe that one of the most powerful aspects of prayer is not us getting what we want done, but about us learning what is truly in the heart of God, about his will for our lives and the world. Jesus powerfully expressed this when he prayed one of the greatest unanswered prayers in the Bible:

> Father, if you are willing, take this cup from me; yet not my will, but yours be done. (Luke 22:42)

Let's be people who seek, through prayer, to be constantly deepening our relationship with God our Father.

THROUGH THE SON

Then we need to understand that this relationship with the Father is only possible 'through Jesus'. That it is his death and resurrection which has made it possible for us to come into a place where we can pray, where we can have a relationship with God. That he has made a way to know God where there was no way to know him.

But even more than that, we need to understand that we are now clothed in the righteousness of Jesus. That as adopted children in God's family we are now inheritors of all that was due to Jesus through his perfect life and death. That means that now when God the Father looks at us he literally sees Jesus, and that we can now approach God with incredible boldness and confidence, not because of anything we have done but because of what he has done. As the writer to the Hebrews puts it:

> Therefore, brothers and sisters, since we have confidence to enter the Most Holy Place by the blood of Jesus, by a new and living way opened for us through the curtain, that is, his body, and since we have a great priest over the house of God, let us draw near to God with a sincere heart and with the full assurance that faith brings, having our hearts sprinkled to cleanse us from a guilty conscience and having our bodies washed with pure water. (Hebrews 10:19–22)

That confidence should give us a boldness to ask God for the most amazing things, believing that as our Father his heart now is to bless us and delight in us. But a confidence and boldness that flows not from who we are, but from what Jesus has done for us.

BY THE SPIRIT

Then finally we see that prayer is by the Spirit. Later on we're going to look at how God wants us to be filled with the Holy Spirit. Let's just say for now that one of the reasons for the Spirit coming is to help us to pray. Paul writes to the church in Rome:

> In the same way, the Spirit helps us in our weakness. We do not know what we ought to pray for, but the Spirit himself intercedes for us through wordless groans. (Romans 8:26)

INDIVIDUAL PRAYER

Prayer starts with us as individuals connecting with God. As we've already seen, Jesus said:

> But when you pray, go into your room, close the door and pray to your Father, who is unseen. Then your Father, who sees what is done in secret, will reward you. (Matthew 6:6)

Each one of us needs to develop our own personal prayer life with God. To be living life as a constant, ongoing conversation with God. Talking to him about everything that happens. Involving him in all the decisions, in all the good and the bad things that happen in our days. Repenting quickly when we mess up, praying for direction when we need it, thanking him when good stuff happens.

I think that will look different for each one of us. For me I love to pray outdoors, walking on my own with our dog (and hopefully without too many other people around!). I feel I connect much more powerfully in that context than on my own in a room. Wherever it is, we need to rediscover solitude, finding time on our own alone with God.

COMMUNITY PRAYER

Prayer also needs to be something we gather to do as a community. The start of the Lord's prayer is not 'My Father' but 'Our Father'. Prayer is about a community relating to God, not just a bunch of individuals.

I would hope that means that as we meet informally as individuals we can slip in and out of prayer. If I meet someone in the church who is unemployed, sick, feeling low, has a business which is in difficulty or is struggling in some other way, I want to pray for them there and then, rather than doing that thing of saying 'I'll pray for you' and then never actually doing it. Much better to do it straight away, and open the door to God answering straight away too.

We will also look to pray in all of our gatherings, whether they are on a Sunday, in a Lifegroup, in a planning meeting or in our homes. Again not as some moment where someone stops and announces 'now we are going to pray', but as something we can do very easily and naturally.

Then we will have specific times when we gather to pray. That might be a church-wide prayer meeting or prayer for a specific issue or ministry. We will pray for protection, for breakthrough, for direction, and in the context of prayer be expecting to hear from God too.

FASTING

Jesus also clearly saw a powerful place for the discipline of fasting. He himself fasted, and when he spoke of his followers fasting he spoke of 'when you fast' rather than 'if you fast'.[58] But as with prayer we need to make sure that our fasting is fasting which connects with God. Not the fasting Isaiah speaks out against in Isaiah 58, which was more about an external show rather than humbling oneself before God, but the sort of fasting which as Isaiah says will 'set the oppressed free and break every yoke'.[59]

ONE FINAL THOUGHT

There is so much more I could say on prayer – perhaps one day we'll write a separate book on it. But here is what I believe is the core. There is a prayer in which we can totally miss God, where we think we're being spiritual, but actually we're just being religious and going through the motions.

But then there is a prayer which is living, active, dynamic, honest, real and faith-filled and which genuinely connects us with the creator of the universe. It is a prayer where we'll hear from God, even when what he says isn't necessarily what we want to hear, and it's a prayer which will ultimately connect us more deeply to him and his purposes in our lives.

Too Busy Not to Pray
Bill Hybels

A very practical, down to earth book on how to develop a life of prayer.

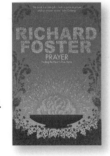

Prayer
Richard Foster

Another profound but accessible book on how to grow in the practice of prayer.

Prayer That Brings Revival
David Yonggi Cho

I read this book not long after I became a Christian, and its impact is still with me today. Yonggi Cho argues strongly for prayer being the key to seeing breakthrough in every area of our lives.

Your faith
has saved you;
go
in peace

SARAH

When you meet Sarah today she is a warm, confident lady, working hard to bring up her son, and full of life and hope. Turn back the clock a few years, though, and you would meet a very different person. During my childhood, my father suffered from a mental illness, causing him to be abusive towards his family. This dynamic shaped my life and I found myself craving intimacy and security, something to paste over the hurt. I would try to forget about life and hide my emotions by working hard, striving for material things, and partying. The highlight of my week would be the weekends, when I would be going out with friends, getting drunk and doing the odd recreational drug.

I was in an unhappy long-term relationship when I found myself pregnant, a wonderful delight. But the baby stopped growing at thirty weeks, prompting a premature birth and a frightening sequence of events. My little boy became unstable and was close to death. Knowing there was absolutely nothing I could do other than love him, I prayed and prayed, probably for the first time in my life.

Lewis made a remarkable recovery and I tried to piece my world back together, but my relationship with my partner fell apart. My drinking got out of control again and I escaped life by using marijuana more frequently. I became good friends with someone who was deeply involved in the occult. Looking back now I see I was seeking something deep inside, and I really believed there was more to life than the visible. The promise I'd made at my son's christening kept coming back to me, but when I went to a church I felt like an outsider and had an overwhelming feeling of guilt.

A conversation I'd had about the Alpha course kept springing to mind, so I decided to find out what it was all about. Though I was interested in learning the whole meaning of life, I genuinely thought it wouldn't have any effect on me. I went to the course wanting to prove to myself that it was all a load of rubbish, but I encountered God in ways that were both real and life-changing.

I had a dream where I was calling for Jesus to help me, and when I woke he was standing right there beside me, giving me complete peace and comfort. The proof just kept flowing. My boy was having issues at school so I asked Jesus to deal with them. Two days later his teacher asked what I'd done to him as he was like a different child! The more I asked for proof the more I got it, so I put my hands up and said, 'I believe you, I'm yours!"

I started going to the Kerith Centre on Sundays. From the moment I walked through the door on my first Sunday, I was made to feel welcome. I didn't know anybody, but people introduced themselves to me and looked out for me. As I got more involved in the community I found that people accepted me for who I was, there was no judgement, and I was truly allowed to be myself.

Where before I had found guilt and shame, I was now met with love and belonging, and this accepting environment was a key factor in my integrating fully and building my relationship with God. I have since begun working as a debt coach for Christians Against Poverty and started up a single parents' group.

It's been an emotional rollercoaster, but I know now that God was always looking out for me and loving me, and he always will be. As I keep saying to Jesus: 'The words "thank you" just don't seem enough!'

justice

Is not this the kind of fasting I have chosen:
to loose the chains of injustice and untie the cords of the yoke, to
set the oppressed free and break every yoke?
Is it not to share your food with the hungry and to provide the
poor wanderer with shelter - when you see the naked, to clothe
them, and not to turn away from your own flesh and blood?
Then your light will break forth like the dawn, and your healing
will quickly appear; then your righteousness will
go before you, and the glory of the LORD will be your rear guard.
Then you will call, and the LORD will answer;
you will cry for help, and he will say: Here am I.

(Isaiah 58:6–9)

When I became a Christian, having never been to church before, I had
this idea that all churches were basically the same. I quickly came to
realise that this simply wasn't true. There were many ways you could
categorise churches into different types based on worship style,
denomination, age of the congregation, where they met, the use of
the gifts of the Holy Spirit and many other factors. But one of the
clearest differentiations was how churches approached the issue of
being a force for justice, of speaking up for and practically helping the
poor, the disadvantaged and the marginalised in society.

Some of the churches I observed, which were also the sort
of church I went to and which might be grouped under the evangelical
banner, were primarily focussed on preaching the gospel, on reaching
out to lost people with the good news of Jesus Christ. They seemed
to consider getting involving in justice as at best an optional extra, and

at worst a dangerous distraction to preaching the gospel.

Other churches, which might be thought of as being more liberal in their theology, focussed more on what is often called the social gospel. Most of their energies went into demonstrating the love of Jesus through practical acts of service – feeding the poor, giving shelter to the homeless, caring for the environment and engaging with politics, but with little emphasis on the gospel.

Now of course this is a huge generalisation, but I think it's one which is truer than we might like to admit. Tim Keller put it this way in speaking about his book Generous Justice:

'Those who are all about justification by faith alone are not usually about justice. And those who are all about justice usually are not about justification by faith alone. I think that is a big mistake.' [60]

We are passionate here about the gospel (hopefully you've already picked that up). Passionate about creating the environment where people can hear the message of the good news of Jesus Christ, understand the depth of their own sinfulness, and come into a life-changing relationship with him.

But we also believe that if someone has fully grasped the gospel, if they've truly come into that transforming relationship with God, then it will naturally cause them to live a life of justice. That's what Isaiah is arguing in the passage quoted at the start of this chapter. Fasting was a sign of repentance, of humbling yourself before God and getting your relationship right with him. Isaiah is saying that if the Israelites had truly done that, then it would show itself by their works of justice, by their care for the vulnerable in their society, practically meeting the needs of the naked, the poor and the hungry. The fact that it isn't manifested in such a way shows that their hearts really aren't right with God.

In the New Testament James makes the same argument when he talks about faith without works. He says:

What good is it, my brothers and sisters, if someone claims to have faith but has no deeds? Can such faith save them? Suppose a brother or a sister is without clothes and daily food. If one of you says to them, 'Go in peace; keep warm and well fed,' but does nothing about their physical needs, what good is it? In the same way, faith by itself, if it is not accompanied by action, is dead. (James 2:14–17)

He isn't arguing that faith isn't important, or that in any sense our works can earn us a relationship with God. But what he is saying is that if we genuinely have faith, then that will be demonstrated in the way we live our lives, and in particular in the practical ways in which we treat the poor and disadvantaged people around us.

We need to be clear about two things here:

1 Doing social justice is different and distinct from preaching the gospel, and we must never confuse the two. You don't have to be a Christ follower to get involved in justice; in fact there are many non-believing individuals and organisations doing fantastic justice work. But preaching the gospel and showing people the way to a relationship with God is our unique contribution to society. We are the only people who have been entrusted with the gospel, and we must never water it down or confuse it with doing justice.

2 We mustn't do social justice simply as a means to making our preaching of the gospel more effective. We must seek to do justice because it is the right thing to do, flowing out of our lives changed by the power of the gospel. Now it is undoubtedly true that meeting people's practical needs will in most cases make them more open to the gospel, and we mustn't be afraid as we help people to tell them about Jesus and how they can come into a relationship with him, but that should never be our primary motivation in helping them. We stand up for justice because God is a God of justice.

So let's take a look at some of the implications of all this.

PERSONAL IMPLICATIONS

Living a life of justice starts not with what our church does but with how we live our everyday lives. Let me give some practical examples of things we can all do:

⮊ Be aware of the people in our streets who need help. Is there a single mum who needs a babysitter, an elderly person who needs some company or a new family who have just moved into the area and need some help working out where everything is? If so then put yourself out to help them.

⮊ In our schools, colleges or workplaces let's be looking out for people who are lonely, being bullied, struggling with their work or going through a hard time, and let's be willing to befriend them, stand with them and speak up on their behalf.

- If you know of people in your church community who are struggling then don't wait for 'the church', as some central organisation, to meet their needs but realise that you are 'the church' and need to do what you can. That might be buying some food and leaving it on their doorstep, putting an envelope with some money in through their door, looking out for them on a Sunday and asking how they are, or pointing them at some resources which might help them.

- When you're out and about buy the Big Issue and help the homeless get themselves back on their feet. Leave generous tips in restaurants, realising that many of the waiters and waitresses will be on minimum wage, relying on their tips to make a living.

- Everywhere you go seek to live out the great commandment to 'love the Lord your God.. and.. love your neighbour as yourself'.[61]

CHURCH IMPLICATIONS
Paul writes to Timothy that:

> Anyone who does not provide for their relatives, and especially for their own household, has denied the faith and is worse than an unbeliever. (1 Timothy 5:8)

There is a danger when we begin to think of the church getting involved in justice that we think of the people 'out there'. I believe that we need to start not 'out there' but 'in here' and make sure there are no poor people in the church before we start worrying about the poor outside the church. It's interesting that in passages such as Matthew 25:31–46, which people sometimes use to set a context for doing social justice, Jesus is actually talking about meeting the needs of 'brothers and sisters', of those already in the family of believers, and how what differentiates the sheep and the goats is how we treat other believers. As we've already seen James makes the same argument.

In Acts 4 we read:
> All the believers were one in heart and mind. No one claimed that any of their possessions was their own, but they shared everything they had. With great power the apostles continued to testify to the resurrection of the Lord Jesus. And God's grace was so powerfully at work in them all that there were no needy persons among them. For from time to time those who owned land or houses sold them, brought the money from the sales and put it at the apostles' feet, and it was distributed to anyone who had need. (Acts 4:32–35)

I find it fascinating that the evidence that 'God's grace was so powerfully at work in them' was not the amazing miracles which were undoubtedly taking place, or the remarkable conversion growth they were seeing, but God's justice being worked out in their own community such that there were 'no needy persons among them'. In using these words, Luke (who wrote Acts) echoes a passage in Deuteronomy 15 where Moses is setting out God's laws for the nation of Israel and says 'there need be no poor people among you'.[62]

God's desire is for a community on earth that reflects his rule and his perfect and just kingdom. Today that community is the church, and if we were truly living out and expressing his kingdom then we would live together in such a way that none of us would be poor. For a moment in time, the early church achieved this. For us now, in a world where there is an increasing gap between rich and poor, there being no poor in our community would mark us out dramatically.

That means we aim for Kerith to be a community where the needs of everyone in the church community are being met. That starts with us as individuals caring for one another, but when that provision is insufficient we have central funds and resources available to help people, just as the early church did. To this end we set aside a proportion of all our income to help those in need within our community, as well as making sure resources such as Christians Against Poverty (CAP), the Foodbank and money management courses are as available to those inside the church as to those outside.

LOCAL IMPLICATIONS

Our first responsibility is to make sure that care for the poor is worked out within the church community. But beyond that we do have a responsibility to the wider community. Jesus makes that clear in the parable of the good Samaritan,[63] which is told in response to an expert in the law who asks Jesus 'who is my neighbour?' In the parable a man is robbed and left for dead by the side of the road. Two religious people deliberately ignore him, but a Samaritan, considered by the Jews to be a second-class citizen, stops and helps the man. Jesus then tells the expert in the law that we are to be a neighbour to anyone in need of mercy.

Locally this means we will seek to meet the practical needs of people in our community. We want to be such a church that if we ceased to exist then the local community would notice the difference, and not just because there would be more parking on a Sunday!

Our philosophy in reaching out to our local community has been driven by a number of guiding principles:

WE SEEK to focus our energies on a few chosen projects. We could easily dissipate our effectiveness by taking on too many areas of service. Instead we try to focus our resources on a limited number of activities and provide much deeper resources in those areas where we are involved.

WE SEEK to do things which nobody else in our community is doing. That way we can make a much bigger impact and fill gaps rather than just replicating what somebody else is already doing.

WE SEEK to work in partnership with organisations, so that we can benefit from their experience, learn from their mistakes and focus on actually helping people rather than the mechanics of the ministry, and they can help us to make better use of our limited financial resources. Our partnerships with Christians Against Poverty and the Trussell Trust would be great examples of this.

WE SEEK to work alongside other organisations in our community who are working for justice, both Christian and secular. That means having Foodbank vouchers distributed by over forty other agencies in Bracknell Forest and CAP getting referrals from many of those agencies too. It also means referring people to other agencies which have more expertise in a particular area than us.

NATIONAL IMPLICATIONS

As well as doing what we can to support organisations like CAP and the Trussell Trust in what they are doing, we realise that some justice issues are better tackled by national Christian organisations. An example of this would be our working with Hope for Justice, a charity seeking to eradicate human trafficking in the UK.

We also seek to be a resource base for other churches in the UK, helping them in any way we can to be more effective at bringing justice to their local community.

INTERNATIONAL IMPLICATIONS

The fact that someone is on the other side of the world doesn't stop them from being our neighbour, and we realise that as part of the church in the resourced first world, we have a responsibility to meet needs in the under-resourced world. In 2008 we felt God called us to get involved in the issue of HIV/AIDS, as a result of which we have engaged with a rural community in Zambia called Serenje. We are involved in a five-year project helping children affected by AIDS to complete their education, providing seed and goats for farmers, and training volunteers and church leaders to meet the needs of those living with HIV/AIDS. That project has now expanded to include schools around Bracknell linking with schools in Serenje, an operating theatre in the hospital in Serenje being equipped, and a dormitory for 100 secondary school girls being built.

All of the principles we apply locally we are also seeking to work out internationally. We realise that we can't meet all of the vast need in the third world, but we can seek to make a major difference in one community. We're attempting to do some things in that community which no one else is attempting. And we are working in partnership with both Tearfund and the Evangelical Fellowship of Zambia, who have far more idea of what they are doing than we do.

Beyond that we've had a heart not just to link our church with the churches in Serenje, but to link the community of Bracknell Forest with the community of Serenje. So far we've already seen links between schools and links between hospitals, with incredibly beneficial effects both in the UK and in Zambia.

SUGGESTED RESOURCES

Generous Justice
Timothy Keller

This is the best book I've ever read giving a biblical understanding of how the gospel and justice flow together, and how they should each find their unique place in the life of the believer.

Nevertheless
John Kirkby

John tells the story of Christians Against Poverty, the debt counselling service we partner with, which so embodies these twin goals of preaching the gospel and practically meeting people's needs.

Letter from a Birmingham Jail
Martin Luther King Jr

This letter was written by King from the city jail in Birmingham, Alabama, after he had been arrested for non-violent protest, in response to a letter from eight white clergy criticising him for his actions. It should, I think, be required reading for anyone serious about seeing the church get involved in the social issues of our day. The letter can be found in numerous places on the internet.

nations

I will make you into a great nation and I will bless you;
I will make your name great, and you will
be a blessing.
I will bless those who bless you, and whoever
curses you I will curse;
and all peoples on earth will be blessed through you.

(Genesis 12:2–3)

When God first called Abram (before he changed his name to Abraham) he was very clear that the aim was not just to bless Abraham and the people associated with him, or even just to make them into a mighty nation. God's plan was that through Abraham and his descendants every nation on earth would experience the goodness, tenderness and mercy of God.

When he gave us the great commission, Jesus made it clear that we are now the inheritors of that promise and that goal:

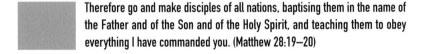

Therefore go and make disciples of all nations, baptising them in the name of the Father and of the Son and of the Holy Spirit, and teaching them to obey everything I have commanded you. (Matthew 28:19–20)

It doesn't seem that this call to the nations always comes naturally or easily for us. Take the early church. In Acts 2:42–47 we read about what seems to be an amazing local church, and what many would hold up to be a model of how church should be today.

They devoted themselves to the apostles' teaching and to fellowship, to the breaking of bread and to prayer. Everyone was filled with awe at the many wonders and signs performed by the apostles. All the believers were together and had everything in common. They sold property and possessions to give to anyone who had need. Every day they continued to meet together in the temple courts. They broke bread in their homes and ate together with glad and sincere hearts, praising God and enjoying the favour of all the people. And the Lord added to their number daily those who were being saved.

There are so many things which are great about this church, and so much we can learn from it. Miracles, daily salvation, incredible fellowship, the centrality of prayer and scripture, sacrificial generosity. And yet consider this. The thing which Jesus has commanded them to do after his resurrection, to go to the nations (or even just to go to Judea and Samaria – see Acts 1:8), they are failing to do.

In fact in the end God has to send persecution to the church in order to get them out of their cosy Jerusalem bubble. We read in Acts 8:1 that after Stephen is stoned to death, with Paul giving his approval:

On that day a great persecution broke out against the church in Jerusalem, and all except the apostles were scattered throughout Judea and Samaria.

This leads to the church finally beginning to fulfil its commission to go to the nations, as we read in verse 4 that:

Those who had been scattered preached the word wherever they went.

We must make sure that we don't have the same blind spot as the early church, that we never become so transfixed by what is happening in our local area that we lose sight of our mandate to go to the nations. We've tried to embody that in our vision statement:

'**To be a rapidly growing community of followers of Jesus Christ, contributing to local, national and international life**'.

This international focus will have a number of outworkings.

LOCALLY

We live in a society where we are surrounded by people from other nations. That means we don't need to get on a plane and fly to another nation to reach the nations. Instead we can reach the nations simply by talking to our neighbour, our work colleague, the dad at the kids' football or the mum at the school gate. Often that will mean us stepping out of our comfort zones, in the language of Bill Hybels 'walking across the room', [64] and talking to someone different from us. Finding out where they are from, listening to their story and sharing our lives with them.

Actually reaching people locally can be the most effective way of reaching nations. When people from other nations get saved here, then if they go back to their nations they will be far more effective in bringing the gospel than we could ever have been as outsiders.

We must also recognise the nations in our church community. We'll look more at this when we look at diversity, but just to say that last time we counted there were forty-three different nations represented in our church community. Our goal must be to see all of those nations coming together as a declaration of how God wants to unite the nations.

NATIONALLY

After thinking about Jerusalem, Jesus called the disciples to think about the places beyond the immediate reach of their church, to go to Judea and Samaria. Similarly we want to have a national impact which goes beyond the immediate boundaries of the people we reach. This will be expressed in a number of ways.

➯ We host conferences with a heart not just to bless our own church community but also to bless the wider church in our nation. Some of these, such as the Willow Creek Global Leadership Summit, will be run in partnership with other organisations. Others will be conferences which we organise ourselves.

➯ We support other churches and church plants, whether through direct financial support, by providing leadership training and input, by providing preachers and speakers, by training their leaders through the Kerith Academy or by providing other types of support and encouragement.

➯ We host church leadership teams wanting to come and learn from how we are doing church.

➯ We work to support the work of other national organisations, such as Christians Against Poverty, Hope for Justice, Tearfund and the Trussell Trust, in what they are seeking to do in the UK. This might include hosting conferences and events for them or supporting them financially.

- We seek to give away anything we have which might be useful to other churches. That includes making all of our music, CDs, graphics and sermon series freely available to anyone who can make use of them.

INTERNATIONAL

Having said all that, we do still want to reach other nations.

We want to help build churches in other nations. Churches which will have strong local leaders, not leaders parachuted in from the UK, and which although they may share many of our values will also understand their own cultural context and what it means to build a church in that environment. In some countries we work with churches in the Newfrontiers family of churches, and in others we work with churches from other groups and denominations.

And as discussed in the previous chapter, we also want to be involved in bringing justice in other nations.

KINGDOM MINDED, NOT KERITH MINDED

An important principle to grasp in all of this is that God has called us to be kingdom minded, not in any way to be trying to promote Kerith or build a Kerith empire. Jesus taught us to pray 'your kingdom come, your will be done'. It is our job to do everything we can to advance the kingdom of God, wherever it is, however it is expressed and regardless of whether or not it has our name attached to it. That means that if a church down the road, or on the other side of the world, flourishes because of something we have done, then their success is our success. In fact even if we had nothing to do with it then it's still our success, as we're all part of the same kingdom.

WHAT ABOUT YOU?

Here are some ideas as to how you, as an individual, can have an international focus:

- Reach out to your international neighbour in your street, at work or at the school gate.

- Be the first on a Sunday to reach out across the national divide and initiate conversations with people from other nations.

- Pray for the nations. Jesus told us that his house should be a house of prayer for all nations, so next time you see a nation featured on the news, or are reminded of nations we work with, pray for the churches and the leaders in that country.

➲ By giving regularly on a Sunday you are already involved in the nations, as a proportion of the money you give is going to churches and projects in other nations.

➲ Go on an overseas trip, or support someone you know to go. Flights to many of the places where we are working in Europe are getting cheaper and cheaper, to such an extent that a trip to one of those churches should be affordable for many of us.

➲ Host somebody coming from another nation to visit us, or pick them up from the airport. We regularly have international visitors, many of whom need hosting. If you've got the space in your home it's a great way to get to know them.

WE ARE BLESSED TO BE A BLESSING

Listen out on Sundays and on my blog (www.simonbenham.com) for opportunities to go on overseas trips and to host people from other nations.

SUGGESTED RESOURCES

Come to the monthly prayer meetings where most months we will pray for the nations.

money

> **No one can serve two masters.**
> **Either you will hate the one and love the other,**
> **or you will be devoted to the one**
> **and despise the other.**
> **You cannot serve both God and money.**

(Matthew 6:24)

Jesus had an incredible way of dealing with money. We see him getting the money to pay the temple tax from the mouth of a fish,[65] telling the rich young ruler to sell everything he had and give to the poor,[66] and appointing a thief as the treasurer for his band of disciples.[67]

And so much of his teaching centred on our attitudes to money and possessions – telling us that we shouldn't store up treasure here on earth but store up treasure in heaven,[68] leaving us in no doubt that it's impossible to serve both God and money,[69] and making the radical claim that it is more blessed to give money away than to receive it.[70]

> **The Bible has twice as many verses about money**
> **as it has on faith and prayer combined.**

Jesus talked more about money than he did on heaven and hell. In fact 15% of Jesus' recorded words relate to the subject of money and possessions. Quite remarkable.

And yet in Christian circles it can often seem like a real taboo to talk about money. It's OK for people to talk about money in relation to politics, in the newspapers, on TV, when discussing football clubs, when deciding which party to vote for in an election, when choosing between two different jobs or when deciding where to go on holiday, but it's somehow wrong to talk about money in church. Which is odd when so much of what is said in the world is frankly nonsense (just look at the army of financial experts who totally failed to predict, or even hint at, the credit crisis we're all living through). The wisdom of Jesus on money has survived 2,000 years of testing, and is still as relevant and as sharp today as it was when he first spoke it.

We want to be as open and as radical about money as Jesus was. You only have to walk around the Kerith Centre (built at a cost of £3.1 million in the middle of a recession with over 98% of the money coming from the congregation) to realise that faith for money, a willingness to talk about money, and sacrificial giving have been part of our history, that they're in our DNA. And that as we look to grow to be a church of thousands which plants other churches of thousands, handling money correctly, and being willing to talk about it openly, is going to be a huge part of our future.

So what does it look like to be a peach community when it comes to money? Well, to explain that we're going to devote two chapters to the subject. In this chapter we're going to look at what Jesus taught us about money and the way we handle it. Then in the next chapter we're going to look at what the Bible and Jesus have to say on the subject of tithing.

JESUS, MONEY AND ME

Let's be clear, we live in a society which worships money and the accumulation of all the things which money can buy. Some of us have now got so much stuff that we can't even fit it all in our homes, so we have to start paying companies to store the possessions we can't fit in but which somehow we can't bear to be without.

When Jesus told us not to store up treasure on earth where rust destroys it and thieves can steal it, he was speaking directly into the heart of the world in which you and I live. His words could never be more true than in our 21st century society. The multi-billion pound advertising industry relies on this root of materialism in the heart of every one of us. We buy the lie that if we just had that car, that house, that phone, that games console, that deodorant, that TV or that holiday then we'd be really satisfied and fulfilled. Time and again every one of us has fallen for it and then, having got that thing, found that there's still something huge missing from our lives.

And time and again we fall for the lie that we can have it all now. That we don't have to wait until we can afford to pay for that thing we really want, but that through the wonders of credit cards and overdrafts and payday loans we can have it now and pay later. That we can cope with the debt, and that at some point in the future something magical will happen which will mean we can pay it all off.

> The Bible sees a very clear link between our spirituality and our attitude to money.

When the crowds asked John the Baptist how they should demonstrate their repentance he told them first to share their clothes and their food with the poor, then he told the tax collectors not to collect any more than they were supposed to, and finally he told the soldiers not to extort money from the people and to be happy with their pay.[71] Jesus told the rich young ruler to sell everything he had[72] and commended Zacchaeus as he sold half of all he had to give to the poor and paid back everyone he had cheated four times over.[73] And in the book of Acts we see the heart of the early disciples being demonstrated by their willingness to give,[74] the hearts of Ananias and Sapphira being shown to be deceitful as they lied about their giving,[75] and the reality of the conversion of the occultists in Ephesus being shown in their willingness to burn their magic books which were worth over 50,000 days' wages.[76]

It was Martin Luther, the great reformer, who said,

'There are three conversions a person needs to experience:
the conversion of the head,
the conversion of the heart,
and the conversion of the wallet.'

Just as Jesus and the early church did, we want to call people to a radically different lifestyle from the world around us when it comes to money. So please don't be surprised if we talk very openly about money. We want to see everyone set free to enjoy the life Jesus has for them, free from the grip of materialism, free from worry and fear, and free to make an impact not just in this world but for eternity.

At the same time we also want to be very clear about some things that Jesus and the Bible don't say about money.

First, the Bible doesn't say that money itself is evil. It is the 'love of money' which Paul says is 'a root of all kinds of evil'.[77] Jesus saw money just as a tool, in the same way as a spade is a tool which can be used either for good (to plant crops) or for evil (to kill somebody). It is man's sinful heart which is the problem, not money in and of itself.

Some Christians have taken on board the idea that money is evil, and believe therefore that we should live in poverty (what is called asceticism). Jesus doesn't call us to seek a life of poverty, or say that following him should mean us not enjoying the material things that this world has to offer. Nowhere does the Bible say that it is better to be poor than to be rich or that God prefers us to be poor. God's heart is to care for and protect the poor, but that is out of his compassion for them, not because he loves poor people more than rich people.

Paul tells us that 'everything God created is good, and nothing is to be rejected if it is received with thanksgiving, because it is consecrated by the word of God and prayer.'[78] Godliness is found not in denying ourselves all that this world has to offer, but understanding that everything is a gift from God and, if understood correctly with thanksgiving and prayer, it is to be enjoyed.

Jesus also didn't say anywhere that it is wrong to have money or possessions, or that it was wrong to seek to earn more money than we need to support our lifestyle. I love the words of John Wesley, who said:

> **Make as much as you can,**
> **save as much as you can and**
> **give as much as you can.**

Jesus encouraged us to use money to advance the kingdom of God – 'use worldly wealth to gain friends for yourselves'. [79]

It's obvious as we read through the book of Acts that there were people in the early church who had significant material and financial resources. The question is not 'do you have money?' but 'does money have you?' That was why Jesus threw out such a strong challenge to the rich young ruler to sell all his possessions. If God has blessed us with the ability to make money then it's right to use that gift to make more money than we need just to survive, so that we can invest it back into the kingdom of God.

On the other hand Jesus doesn't say that if we follow him then we'll automatically be the wealthiest people in society and have the biggest houses and drive the most expensive cars – what some would call a prosperity gospel. I've met Christians who genuinely believe that the size of your bank account is a representation of the size of your faith. I struggle to see how you get to that when Jesus died with his clothes as his only possession, and when the apostle Paul, who didn't seem to be short on faith, wrote:

I know what it is to be in need, and I know what it is to have plenty. I have learned the secret of being content in any and every situation, whether well fed or hungry, whether living in plenty or in want. (Philippians 4:12)

But at the same time it is true that if we put God at the centre of our lives we can expect God to prosper us, not only in our finances but in every area of life.[80] And as Paul says so clearly when writing to the church in Corinth about giving, if we sow generously we can expect to reap generously.[81]

There is so much more that could be said on this whole subject. I'd encourage everyone to get hold of a copy of Randy Alcorn's book Money, Possessions and Eternity which in a very readable way goes into much more detail on living this radically different lifestyle. We haven't got space to cover all of that here, but I do want to finish this chapter with three keys to our living this lifestyle in our peachy community.

BE HONEST

Wherever you're at with your finances I want to encourage you to be honest. First of all be honest with yourself, be honest with God, and then have the courage to be honest with those around you. Part of being a peach community is being willing to take off the masks and to admit that we're all broken people and that none of us have all of this totally sorted.

> Some of you reading this will know deep in your heart that you are gripped by materialism.

That your life and the decisions you make are driven by the desire for a bigger house, a better car, clothes with the right labels on, and that your security is wrapped up in the size of your bank account. Some of you are missing your children growing up because you're so consumed by work and moving up the career ladder so that you can earn more. Some of you know that you can't follow the call of God on your life because what God is calling you to would never pay the salary needed to cover your mortgage.

Others of you will be very aware that your personal finances are in an enormous mess. That you've run up debts which are rapidly getting out of control, that you're not sleeping well at night and you feel deeply ashamed about the situation you're in. You might even be considering suicide. If you're in a mess then please seek help immediately. Talk to one of our Christians Against Poverty debt counselling team, who will be able to help you to map a way to get out of debt.

Whatever your situation, our church community is a safe place to be open about your finances.

BE GENEROUS

The biblical key to breaking the hold of materialism on our lives is an extravagant generosity. That was the key that Jesus knew would unlock the heart of the rich young man: to give it away.

That doesn't necessarily mean giving it all away. Although that was what Jesus demanded of the rich young ruler, when Zacchaeus gave away half of all he had he was commended by Jesus. Jesus doesn't want your money, or need your money; he wants your heart.

Generosity needs to be a lifestyle for each one of us. Maybe it's buying a magazine from the Big Issue seller. Maybe it's when you walk into a bar with your friends being willing to buy the first round. Maybe it's how much of a tip you leave at a restaurant. Maybe it's seeing someone in financial need in your Lifegroup and helping them directly.

And generous giving means sacrificial giving. Giving to a point where the level of our giving affects our lifestyle choices. It doesn't mean just dropping a few pounds in the offering. We'll look more at this in the next chapter.

MANAGE YOUR FINANCES WELL

Thirdly, learn to handle your finances well. The key to that is very simple: to live debt free and to ensure that your income exceeds your expenditure. Paul wrote 'Let no debt remain outstanding, except the continuing debt to love one another'.[82] That also means handling all your money with integrity – be honest with your expense or benefit claims, with your taxes (including VAT), with your bills.

We haven't got time here to give a complete financial planning course. But if you've never had any advice on money management then I can't recommend too highly the CAP Money course which we run on a regular basis. Book yourself on the next one, and put into practice what you hear.

FINAL THOUGHTS

Where are you at with your money? Have you got control of your money or has it got control of you? Has God or materialism got a grip on your heart? Are you living an extravagantly generous life or an incredibly mean life? I pray that God will set you free and prosper you in the whole area of money.

Money, Possessions and Eternity
Randy Alcorn

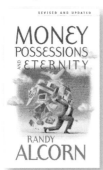

This is quite simply the most thorough and best-written book I've read on what the Bible teaches on finances.

CAP Money Course
I'd encourage everyone, including teenagers and students, to do the CAP money course.
For details visit: **www.kerith.co.uk**

BRIAN & CAROL

Brian and Carol found themselves isolated by debt and desperate for help. Carol tells their story.

It all started when I was working as a driving instructor and also looking after our son, Shannon, who has special needs. My job left me with hardly any money after paying my franchise fee and buying petrol. My husband, Brian, would often be without work as a decorator and we didn't get any help from the DSS as we owned our own house. At one point we were living on £10 a week for food, with nothing left for bills.

I cut ties with all my friends and family because I was so ashamed of our situation. The phone never stopped ringing and threats came in handfuls through the post. If there was any movement outside the house, we would get down on our hands and knees and crawl around the house so the collectors didn't know we were there. Then we received a repossession notice on the house.

I was at my lowest point and thought the only way out was suicide. I tried to talk Brian into a suicide pact so that no one would be left to carry the can. He said there must be another way out and had read an article in the paper about Christians Against Poverty.

When Andy Jackson (Bracknell CAP Centre Manager) came to the house I was hiding in the kitchen, but when Brian brought him through I felt as though a long-lost friend had walked in. He did not judge us or put the blame on anyone.

After we had looked at the paperwork, Andy prayed for us and I physically felt an arm across my shoulders even though I was sitting alone. We saw God working for us from that day on. Brian soon found work and I went for an interview and was given a job straight away. Then Andy worked out a budget for us and CAP became the contact for all our debtors. After a few months, Andy invited us to go on a client break to Disneyland, all expenses paid. We had a wonderful weekend, especially talking to other friends and families in similar situations.

Andy invited me to church and when I walked through the door of the Kerith Centre I felt as though I had come home. A few Sundays later, nothing was going to stop me from giving my life to God. I then went to Alpha and at the away day, I received the Holy Spirit and had the most beautiful inner peace. Brian also committed himself to God and he and Shannon were baptised together.

I was baptised on Easter Sunday. When I came out of the water, I felt as though I was flying. I now know that God is always with us. We still struggle at times and life can be hard, but we have an inner strength that's greater than anything in this world. Our lives are now worth living for the beauty that surrounds us and the help that we can give to others, no matter how small.

tithing

Each of you should give what you have decided in
your heart to give, not reluctantly or under compulsion,
for God loves a cheerful giver.

(2 Corinthians 9:7)

We talked in the last chapter about generosity, sacrificial financial giving, being the key to breaking the hold of materialism in our lives. But that raises the question: where do I start? Is putting £5 into the offering basket every week enough, or do I need to follow the example of the rich young ruler, sell everything I have and give the money to the poor? As in the rest of life, God has given us the Bible as our guide for living, so in this chapter we're going to look at what the Bible has to say about giving, and in particular the biblical principle of tithing.

TITHING IN THE OLD TESTAMENT
The earliest reference to tithing is in Genesis 14 (before the giving of the law to Moses) where we read:

> Then Melchizedek king of Salem brought out bread and wine. He was priest of God Most High, and he blessed Abram, saying, 'Blessed be Abram by God Most High, Creator of heaven and earth, and praise be to God Most High, who delivered your enemies into your hand.' Then Abram gave him a tenth of everything. (Genesis 14:18–20)

Abram gives to Melchizedek a tenth (a tithe) of everything he has. In Hebrews 7 we read that Melchizedek was a representation of Jesus, and that Abram is in effect giving a tenth of everything back to God.

The idea of tithing is then developed in Leviticus 27:

> A tithe of everything from the land, whether grain from the soil or fruit from the trees, belongs to the LORD; it is holy to the LORD. Whoever would redeem any of their tithe must add a fifth of the value to it. Every tithe of the herd and flock—every tenth animal that passes under the shepherd's rod—will be holy to the LORD. (Leviticus 27:30–32)

Other passages develop how the tithes were to be used: Numbers 18:21–24, Deuteronomy 12:5–17, Deuteronomy 14:22–23. Some have argued that there were actually three different tithes which were to be paid. 10% to the Levites,[83] 10% for use in the feasts and the temple,[84] and a further 10% every three years which went to the poor and outsiders,[85] making a total tithe of 23%. However, scholars disagree on whether this 23% was ever actually practised.

What is clear is that, as with the rest of the requirements of the law, the people struggled ever to live up to the requirements of tithing. The prophets rebuked the people for their failure to tithe,[86] and when the nation repented under the leadership of Hezekiah one of the first results was an enthusiastic return to tithing:

> As soon as the order went out, the Israelites generously gave the firstfruits of their grain, new wine, olive oil and honey and all that the fields produced. They brought a great amount, a tithe of everything. (2 Chronicles 31:5)

TITHING IN THE NEW TESTAMENT

Let's take a look at the two times Jesus is recorded speaking on the subject of tithing.

In Matthew 23:23 (and repeated in Luke 11:42) we hear Jesus rebuking the Pharisees:

> Woe to you, teachers of the law and Pharisees, you hypocrites! You give a tenth of your spices - mint, dill and cumin. But you have neglected the more important matters of the law - justice, mercy and faithfulness. You should have practised the latter, without neglecting the former.

The Pharisees were so focussed on keeping all of the law that they even tithed the herbs they grew in their gardens, yet they missed the more important issues to God – justice, mercy and faithfulness. Notice that Jesus doesn't say they shouldn't tithe, but that as well as tithing they should have done all the other stuff. This isn't a direct indication that Christians should tithe, as Jesus is speaking here to Jews trying to get to God by obeying the law, but it does show that Jesus saw tithing as a requirement of the law.

This is then taken further in the parable of the tax collector in Luke 18:

> To some who were confident of their own righteousness and looked down on everyone else, Jesus told this parable: 'Two men went up to the temple to pray, one a Pharisee and the other a tax collector. The Pharisee stood by himself and prayed: "God, I thank you that I am not like other people - robbers, evildoers, adulterers - or even like this tax collector. I fast twice a week and give a tenth of all I get."
> 'But the tax collector stood at a distance. He would not even look up to heaven, but beat his breast and said, "God, have mercy on me, a sinner."
> 'I tell you that this man, rather than the other, went home justified before God. For all those who exalt themselves will be humbled, and those who humble themselves will be exalted.' (Luke 18:9–14)

The Pharisee is full of himself, using 'I' four times in his prayer and thinking that his tithing has earned him God's approval. This is such a deceptive trap for us to fall into as we go on in our relationship with God, to begin to believe that it is our good works rather than Jesus' death in our place which makes us acceptable to God. To slip into law rather than grace.

And like so many in coconut communities, the Pharisee looks down on the tax collector who, rather than bragging about how great he is, is willing to humble himself before God.

The rest of the New Testament writers have nothing to say directly about tithing, other than the passage we've already referred to in Hebrews 7, which tells us much about Jesus but little about tithing!

GRACE AND TITHING

So how are we to understand the Old Testament principle of tithing, which Jesus reinforced, in a New Testament era?

We start by affirming that in Jesus we live under grace, not under law. This is so key for us to grasp. Under the law tithing was one of the things they had to do to earn God's approval and meet the requirements of the law. Under grace Jesus has done everything that could ever need to be done to earn us God's approval and he has fully met the requirements of the law. Let's be clear: if you never tithe in your life God won't love you any less, and if you give away everything you have God won't love you any more.

We need also to remember that in grace Jesus didn't come

to abolish the law, but to fulfil the law, and give us the heart surgery which gives us the power to live beyond the law.[87] Thus in the sermon on the mount we see Jesus taking the commandments of the law, and showing us that grace always takes us beyond the law.

Erwin McManus, who leads Mosaic Church in Los Angeles, puts it very clearly in his book Unstoppable Force as he records this conversation with somebody thinking of joining Mosaic:

> I was sitting on the hearth of the fireplace with an individual who was considering becoming a part of Mosaic. He turned to me and asked me if Mosaic was a law church or a grace church. It was pretty obvious to me that he was setting a trap, so I thought that I would go ahead and jump in. I said 'Well, of course, we're a grace church.' 'I thought so,' he replied. 'I was concerned that you were one of those law churches that told people they had to tithe.'
>
> 'Oh no,' I said. 'We're a grace church. The law says, "Do not murder." Grace says you don't even have to have hatred in your heart; you can love your enemy. The law says, "Do not commit adultery," but grace says you don't even have to have lust in your heart for another woman. The law says, "Give 10 percent," but grace always takes us beyond the law. You can give 20, 30, or 40 percent. We would never stop you from living by grace.' [88]

We are a grace church too! That means that in an era of grace, tithing isn't abolished but becomes merely a starting point, a baseline to begin our lives from.

The ESV Study Bible puts it like this: 'Rather than stipulating a fixed amount the New Testament places an emphasis on generous, abundant, cheerful giving ... So while Christians are not obligated to give a fixed amount, it is hard to imagine that God expects people of the new covenant to give any less than the 10% tithe in the old covenant.'[89]

The idea of tithing in an era of grace has a number of major implications.

1 First of all it means that tithing should no longer be a requirement but a joy. We no longer give because we are instructed to, but we give in response to a God who has already given us everything. God lavished his grace on us, and our giving is just a small response to what God has already given to us. Paul expresses the heart with which we should give when he says:

> Each of you should give what you have decided in your heart to give, not reluctantly or under compulsion, for God loves a cheerful giver. (2 Corinthians 9:7)

This is something between you and God. Nobody is going to demand that you give in order to be part of our church community. You need to decide what you are going to give, and then give it cheerfully.

2 Secondly, in an era of grace, tithing becomes not a goal to attain but a starting line to begin from. It's not that we spend our whole lives trying to build up to giving 10%, perhaps increasing by another percentage point every few years hoping that before we die we will reach the magic 10%, but instead we start with 10% and then see where God will take us from there. For Catrina and me, we set aside a regular amount we give to the church, which is more than 10% of our combined income, but on top of that we regularly give to a number of charities and causes, as well as setting aside money every month to give to people in need within our church community.

3 This brings us on to the third point, which is that for most of us tithing is a faith issue. Very few of us will ever have enough money that we can 'afford' to tithe, that we can give away 10% without that being a major chunk of our disposable income. The Bible tells us that 'without faith it is impossible to please God',[90] and for most of us the decision to tithe will come down to a faith issue. Do I trust God enough that if I tithe he will make sure I don't get into debt and will instead flourish? Interestingly the only time God tells us to test him is over the issue of tithing:

> 'Bring the whole tithe into the storehouse, that there may be food in my house. Test me in this,' says the LORD Almighty, 'and see if I will not throw open the floodgates of heaven and pour out so much blessing that there will not be room enough to store it.' (Malachi 3:10)

I first took that adventure of faith when I was at university. I had just got my first grant cheque for £600 and then heard my first ever sermon on tithing. My initial thought was 'I can't afford to do this'. But then I began to ask the question 'If instead my grant cheque was £666, so that after I'd tithed it I'd then be left with £600, would I then think I could afford it?' The answer was no, and I realised there and then the question was not one of affordability, but of faith. I wrote out a cheque to my local church for £60 and have been tithing ever since.

I love how Mark Batterson from National Community Church in Washington puts it in his book Wild Goose Chase:

'tithing is not just good stewardship, it turns money management into a financial adventure'. [91]

OTHER IMPLICATIONS OF GRACE

Grace has other implications on our giving.

First of all it means that we don't tithe in order to earn God's approval, or as some sort of cosmic insurance policy against things going wrong in our lives. I know people who have tithed and even double tithed for many years and then got cancer, and others who have never as far as I know given a penny and seem to sail through life moving from one apparent blessing to another. Instead we give freely, joyfully, even hilariously, in response to all that God has done for us.

Grace also means that if there are seasons where we can't tithe, then we don't get into huge condemnation or fear about it. Let me give a couple of examples.

If you get into big debt and work with our CAP debt counselling service, then the budget CAP will negotiate with the people you owe money to won't allow you to tithe. They'll understandably want their money back as quickly as possible and simply won't agree to you giving away 10% to anybody. Proverbs 22:7 tells us that 'the borrower is slave to the lender', and part of the slavery you've got yourself into is that for a season you won't be able to tithe.

I know other people in our church who have become Christians, but have a partner who still hasn't come to faith. In that situation tithing can become a barrier to the partner becoming a Christian, as they feel that all the church is interested in is getting people's money. If your partner objects to you tithing then it may be that, in order to love them and attempt to win them, you decide not to tithe.

> As in all of our lives we need to live under grace, not law.

NET OR GROSS?

People sometimes ask me whether they should tithe on their gross income or their net income. Even the question is confusing as 'net' means different things to different people. For some it's after tax and National Insurance; some also take off pension contributions, mortgage payments, even food bills, utility bills and council tax.

If I'm honest, in my experience this question is usually motivated either out of a desire to work out 'how little can I give?' or out of a life lived under fear of the law and fear that if I 'miss' a portion of my tithe God is going to punish me. Personally, as a starting point, I've always tithed out of my gross income because God has always blessed me on a 'gross' basis, not on a 'net' basis.

The Bible also teaches the principle of our giving out of our firstfruits. In Exodus 23 God says:

> Bring the best of the firstfruits of your soil to the house of the LORD your God. (Exodus 23:19)

If you want to know an organisation which understands the concept of firstfruits take a look at HM Revenue and Customs! Your tax is calculated on the basis of everything you earn. You're not going to get far with them if you try to persuade them that the money for your mortgage or rent shouldn't be included in your tax calculation. They take from the firstfruits, and I believe we should give to God from our firstfruits too.

But in a grace era let's remember that it's not about how much we give, but about the heart we give it with (see Mark 12:41–44).

WHAT SHOULD I GIVE TO?

In the Old Testament tithing was God's plan for funding the priests and the work of the temple, and providing for the poor. Malachi talks about bringing the tithe into the storehouse, the place of God's provision. I believe that we should apply the same principles to the church: that regular giving by the body of believers is God's plan for funding the local church, for paying the salaries of those who work for the church and for providing for the poor both inside and outside the church community. Here is one of the many things Paul wrote to the church in Corinth regarding giving:

> Don't you know that those who serve in the temple get their food from the temple, and that those who serve at the altar share in what is offered on the altar? In the same way, the Lord has commanded that those who preach the gospel should receive their living from the gospel. (1 Corinthians 9:13–14)

So I do believe that your firstfruits, your first giving, should be to the place where you are fed, which hopefully will be your local church. Beyond that give where you want, but our firstfruits should go to our place of provision.

FINAL THOUGHTS

I want to finish with some words which I think should characterise our giving:

Willing and cheerful:
'Each of you should give what you have decided in your heart to give, not reluctantly or under compulsion, for God loves a cheerful giver.'[92] If you're not going to give cheerfully then don't give! Get your heart attitude sorted out first.

Regular:
'On the first day of every week, each one of you should set aside a sum of money...'[93] I would encourage everyone in our community to be a regular giver, not just putting something in the offering when you've got a bit extra or feel like it. For Catrina and me that means giving via a monthly standing order.

Generous:
'In the midst of a very severe trial, their overflowing joy and their extreme poverty welled up in rich generosity. For I testify that they gave as much as they were able, and even beyond their ability.' [95]

Proportionate to your income:
'... set aside a sum of money in keeping with your income ...'[94] Tithing helps us with a baseline for giving in proportion to our income.

Sacrificial:
'They all gave out of their wealth; but she, out of her poverty, put in everything—all she had to live on.' [96]

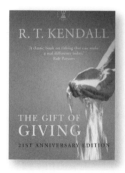

Money, Possessions and Eternity

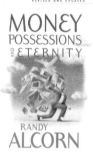

Randy Alcorn

I can't recommend this book strongly enough!

The Gift of Giving
R.T. Kendall

A great blend of biblical teaching on tithing and personal stories of the impact it has had on people's lives.

sex and the peach

> Truly I tell you,
> the tax collectors and the prostitutes
> are entering the kingdom of God
> ahead of you.

(Matthew 21:31)

If you want to tell whether a particular church community is a peach, a coconut or even a tomato, then seeing how they deal with the question of sex will usually give you a very good idea.

> When it comes to sex, as with many other issues,
> we often take one of three approaches.

COCOON ➲ The first is to cocoon ourselves, to be isolationist and to cut ourselves off from the rest of the society. That is often the first reaction of a coconut community, and was certainly the path the Pharisees went down. Cocooning says that the best way to stay morally pure, to live out what the Bible calls us to, is to have nothing to do with people we might consider to be immoral, and to distance ourselves from anyone who doesn't live up to our standards. That was what they expected Jesus to do, and they 'got' him when he didn't. If we go this way we end up seeing the church as a refuge from the world, a place to escape to our own safe community, rather than a refuge for the world, a place where people

far from God can find acceptance and love. Nowhere is this seen more than with sex, where we don't want gay people, people sleeping around, unmarried cohabiting couples or people who have committed adultery messing up our community. Yet we are faced with the example of Jesus and his willingness to engage with exactly the people we might feel tempted to keep at a distance.

The second approach is to confront sin in society, and be very vocal about what we are against. Whether it's Christians protesting about Harry Potter films or homosexuality, we are often known for what we are against rather than what we are for. That flies in the face of what God set out to do, as John writes 'For God did not send his Son into the world to condemn the world, but to save the world through him.' [97] Coconut communities often go for both cocooning and confronting, sitting in their holy huddle lobbing out missiles at the rest of culture – just think of the Pharisees we read about in John 8, who want to stone to death a woman caught committing adultery.

The third approach is to conform, to be no different from the culture around us. That's what happens when a peach becomes a tomato. We so engage with the culture around us that the way we behave is indistinguishable from the people we are trying to reach, and we really have nothing to offer them in terms of showing them a better way to do life.

Jesus called us to a fourth way, not to cocoon, confront or conform, but to be a power for transformation in the world we live in. We see this in his prayer for his disciples:

> My prayer is not that you take them out of the world but that you protect them from the evil one. They are not of the world, even as I am not of it. (John 17:15–16)

Some have summarised that as 'being in the world but not of the world'. I believe that is the challenge that Jesus calls us to when it comes to sex. So how do we go about doing that?

WHAT DID JESUS DO?

We've already seen in the life of Jesus that the way he dealt with people who didn't have it all worked out when it came to sex marked him out as being very different from the religious elite. Just take the woman caught in adultery, whom the Pharisees wanted to stone but Jesus chose to restore.[98] Or the 'sinful' woman who anointed the feet of Jesus and in doing so offended the Pharisee who had invited Jesus into his home.[99]

> **Jesus seemed to have no problem being associated with people who were 'still on a journey' when it came to sex and relationships.**

And consider the way Jesus dealt with the woman at the well, who had already been married five times and was now onto yet another relationship (and was presumably sleeping with the guy she now lived with).[100] Someone like that turning up in a coconut community, if they were brave (or unwise) enough actually to be open about their lifestyle, would almost certainly be told that in order to get their relationship with God on track they must first repent of 'living in sin' before God is going to go any further with them. But Jesus reacted very differently. Rather than rejecting the woman he treated her questions and her life situation with dignity and respect (even after he had a divine revelation of her relationship history), and saw such a change in her that she led a revival amongst the people in her community. At no point did he tell her to get out of the relationship she was in or go back to her previous husband.

I'd also encourage you to think about the genealogy of Jesus. For a Jew the list of one's ancestors was incredibly important, so much so that when Herod the Great wanted to cover up the fact that he was only a half Jew, and so didn't appear in the official genealogies, he had all the records destroyed. Yet as we read the genealogy of Jesus in Matthew 1 we can see that there is something very unusual about it. First of all it contains women, who in both Jewish and Greek culture had no legal rights. But more than that, the women in it include Tamar who committed adultery with her father-in-law,[101] Rahab who was a pagan prostitute[102] and Bathsheba who was seduced by David while she was still married to Uriah.[103] And then of course there were the questions around Jesus' own conception, with the rumour put out by the Jews that he was the illegitimate child of a Roman soldier.

> Through his birth, his life and his genealogy we see that Jesus is happy to be associated not only with men and women, and with Jews and Gentiles, but also with people who don't have it all worked out when it comes to sex.

He has truly come to be a saviour for all, and that includes people who in terms of their sex lives don't fit in with what we think is right. That was very different from the Pharisees, who only seemed to be able to condemn people and point out their faults. As Michael Wilcock says in his commentary on Luke, 'The formal religion of the Pharisees had no real answer to the problem of sin, and could only respond with disapproval and condemnation. But Jesus could actually do away with sin, and in this deepest sense bring salvation and peace.' [104] As we've already seen, being peachy doesn't mean that we're just soft all the way through, with no clear sense of right and wrong. But it does mean that we're willing to accept people without condemnation, whatever their lifestyle and background.

No Perfect People Allowed
John Burke

John deals in detail with some of the issues we have touched on in this chapter, as well as telling inspiring stories of life change in the context of a peach community.

SUGGESTED RESOURCES

be a power for transformation in the world we live in.

TANYA

Tanya (not her real name) thought that church was the last place she would be accepted. I had been in a relationship with an amazing guy for a few years when I felt God calling me back to him. As much as I wanted to rekindle that old relationship that had gone cold, my biggest stumbling block was my perception of Christians. The thought of going to church – the place where Christians all meet – was incredibly scary. Past experiences of church and Christianity had taught me that being a Christian was all about being judgemental. In my view, Christians lived perfect lives in their perfect bubbles and the bits that weren't perfect they never shared. They kept all the rules of the Bible, just like that. Christians took it upon themselves to point out the sin of others and expected everyone to become perfect overnight. Christians could not accept you into their church unless you were willing to make the changes necessary to make their church and, more importantly, them look good.

How refreshing it was to walk into a church where people didn't ask questions or want to judge me for the way I chose to live my life. I remember even trying to push people into making some kind of condemning comment – after all this was what I expected – but instead I got responses like 'God will work out that stuff in his time, just know that he loves you'. At Kerith, my boyfriend and I were accepted, we were made to feel welcome and even invited to social events. What I'm trying to say is that I never felt excluded or that I had to change to belong.

After a few months of my attending church, my friends who weren't Christians started to ask questions about my faith. In particular they couldn't understand how I could go to church and yet be 'living in sin' as they kindly pointed out. The idea of a church that just wanted to accept people and show them love didn't seem to fit into their idea of what church was all about.

OK, so I know sex before/out of marriage isn't right, but in my time of attending Kerith that was never something God put on my heart to deal with. Instead I found parts of my character being challenged and changed, for example being generous not stingy, forgiving people, learning for the first time to love and accept people the way they are, learning to trust a God who is for me and not against me.

Looking back, what would I have done had I experienced condemning Christians who told me how I should live? It would have confirmed my belief that all Christians were judgemental. I wouldn't have come back to church – who would want to go somewhere where they weren't made to feel welcome and accepted? But most importantly, I might not have come back into that relationship with Christ. Today I choose to walk with him, I know that I need him more than anything in my life and am trusting that he will use me to reach those around me. And what about church? Well, I'm now a regular at another large church where I lead a Connect group and serve on the host team. Oh, and my boyfriend? We've just celebrated our second wedding anniversary.

I now know that being a Christian is about loving those around us and bringing people into a relationship with Christ... and that's what I experienced at Kerith. I know I'm not perfect but what I know for certain is that I'm on this journey with Christ for the rest of my life, which is just as well!

sex and the core

> I wrote to you in my letter not to associate with sexually immoral people — not at all meaning the people of this world who are immoral, or the greedy and swindlers, or idolaters. In that case you would have to leave this world.

(1 Corinthians 5:9)

In the last chapter we've seen some of the tension over how we deal with the issue of sex, and how it can mark us out as coconuts, peaches or tomatoes. In this chapter I want to dig a bit deeper into what that means for us practically as Christians living in a sex-obsessed world. How do we deal with believers who mess up when it comes to sex, and how is that different from how we treat and view non-believers? But before that there is another question we need to ask.

WHAT DOES GOD THINK ABOUT SEX?

First of all let's get away from any idea that sex is 'dirty', something that religious people should have nothing to do with and never talk about, and which only exists to produce children.

The Bible is very clear that God invented sex, and that he invented it not only for reproduction but also for our enjoyment.

I'll never forget not long after I first started exploring Christianity, during a less than gripping sermon, leafing through my Bible and discovering for the first time the book Song of Solomon. It's an erotic love poem between a man and a woman, and frankly I was shocked to find verses such as 'Your two breasts are like two fawns, like twin fawns of a gazelle that browse among the lilies' [105] in the middle of this 'holy' book (if you get into the imagery of the book it gets even more intimate than that). Gary Chapman writes 'Obviously, these ancient lovers are finding great pleasure in relating to each other sexually.' [106]

But the Bible is also very clear that sex was created only to be enjoyed in the context of a marriage relationship between one man and one woman.

Genesis 2 tells us 'For this reason a man will leave his father and mother and be united to his wife, and they will become one flesh. The man and his wife were both naked, and they felt no shame.' [107] Sex is the ultimate expression of the two becoming one flesh. Again Gary Chapman writes 'As a husband and wife give themselves to each other sexually, they are building a psychological and spiritual bond that unites their souls at the deepest possible level. Together they can face the challenges of life because they are soul partners. Nothing unites a husband and wife more deeply than making love.' [108]

So followers of Jesus are to avoid sex outside marriage. That means no sex before marriage, and no sex with someone other than your spouse if you are married.

That means that sex outside the context of marriage is wrong. Paul wrote about this to the church in Corinth, a place where sexual immorality was rife, 'Do you not know that he who unites himself with a prostitute is one with her in body? For it is said, "The two will become one flesh."' [109] Having sex isn't just like having a game of squash with someone, a merely physical activity, whatever the proponents of the so-called sexual revolution would have us believe. There is something which happens on a much deeper psychological and spiritual level when two people have sex, which is only intended and only works within the context of marriage. That means that sex outside the context of marriage isn't what God intended.

It also means 'no' to homosexual sex, as a biblical marriage is between one man and one woman. God doesn't say these things to stop us having fun, but because he wants the very best for us.

I know that this raises some huge issues, particularly when it comes to same-sex relationships. It seems clear that there are people who grow up to have an attraction to people of the same sex. There is much debate as to the reason for this, but what is clear biblically is that having a same-sex attraction isn't of itself sin, any more than having an attraction to someone of the opposite sex is sin. What is sin is acting on that attraction and having sex outside marriage. We want to welcome everyone into our community, regardless of their sexual orientation, and to be a safe place for those who in the past may have felt the need to deny or hide their sexuality for fear of rejection or stigma. We want to applaud those people within our community who have a same-sex attraction but have made the courageous decision to live a celibate lifestyle in obedience to God's call on their life.

As a church we want to find ways of supporting all those in our community who have decided to live a celibate life, regardless of their sexual orientation.

RECONCILING TWO IDEAS

So how do we hold onto these two ideas? On the one hand the acceptance which a woman caught in the act of adultery finds from Jesus, and on the other the clear teaching of the Bible on God's standard when it comes to sex?

HIGH EXPECTATIONS FOR BELIEVERS

First of all we want to set the bar very high when it comes to our expectations amongst established Christians in our community. In fact Jesus sets the bar even higher than just not committing adultery.

> You have heard that it was said, 'You shall not commit adultery.' But I tell you that anyone who looks at a woman lustfully has already committed adultery with her in his heart. (Matthew 5:27)

What he's saying is that grace takes us beyond law. The law dealt with the external, but gave us no help in actually keeping the law. In contrast, grace changes us from the inside and through the power of the Holy Spirit gives us strength and a desire actually to want to live God's way.

So when it comes to being sexually pure we set the bar very high, and have high expectations of one another. For me that means being above reproach in both my behaviour and my thinking. Making sure that I never get into a circumstance where I'm on my own with a woman other than Catrina. That I have a group of men whom I trust and who love me enough to hold me to account, to make sure that pornography does not have a grip on me. That I do everything I can to love Catrina as Christ loved the church, and don't let leading the church or anything else in life get in the way of that.

And if people mess up there will be consequences. Depending on what has happened people may be asked to step down from leadership, may not for a season be allowed to preach or lead worship, may have to leave the staff, or may even be asked to go to another church if they've sinned against someone who isn't comfortable with them still being part of our community.

But in all of this our goal, when people fall, is to attempt to restore them with love and grace. As Paul writes:

> Brothers and sisters, if someone is caught in a sin, you who live by the Spirit should restore that person gently. But watch yourselves, or you also may be tempted. (Galatians 6:1)

I've seen too many churches which preach a message of grace but, when someone within the church messes up, either cut them off from the community completely or tell them that God will never be able to use them again and they're going to be 'spoilt goods' for the rest of their life. Grace makes us a church of the second chance (and the third chance, and the fourth chance…). Let's not forget the example of King David, who committed adultery and murder, but on being faced with his sin and genuinely repenting was restored and saw his kingship go from strength to strength.

GRACE FOR PEOPLE FAR FROM GOD

So we set the bar high for Christ followers within our community. But for people new to our community, for people who are still on a journey on their way to discovering Christ, we mustn't make sex, or their relationship status, the big issue. We can't have the same expectations of them as we do of mature believers. Paul puts it this way in The Message translation:

> I wrote you in my earlier letter that you shouldn't make yourselves at home among the sexually promiscuous. I didn't mean that you should have nothing at all to do with outsiders of that sort. Or with crooks, whether blue or white-collar. Or with spiritual phonies, for that matter. You'd have to leave the world entirely to do that! But I am saying that you shouldn't act as if everything is just fine when a friend who claims to be a Christian is promiscuous or crooked, is flip with God or rude to friends, gets drunk or becomes greedy and predatory. You can't just go along with this, treating it as acceptable behaviour. I'm not responsible for what the outsiders do, but don't we have some responsibility for those within our community of believers? God decides on the outsiders, but we need to decide when our brothers and sisters are out of line and, if necessary, clean house. (1 Corinthians 5:9–11 The Message)

Paul makes a huge distinction between the expectations we have of believers and those we have of non-believers. We need to remember that we are building a belong → believe → behave community, so we mustn't expect people to behave before they've believed. If we do that, then we've got back into law and trying to shape people's external behaviour, rather than leading them into a genuine experience of being born again, of being changed from the inside out. John Burke puts it like this in No Perfect People Allowed:

> As leaders ... we must focus first on making sure people are rightly related to God and truly willing to follow Christ. Then we can guide them and direct them to the freedom of following his ways. If we try to force people to morally approximate the gospel before they have the source of life-giving water, we spiritually dehydrate them.[110]

For many people new to our community there will be issues God wants to deal with before he speaks to them about their attitude to sex. Just as with the woman at the well, their relationship status won't be top of the list.

I'm not going to pretend that this isn't very messy. How are we to discern between a couple who are living together, who know it is wrong and need to be faced with their sin, and a couple who, even though they might call themselves Christians, have a whole load of other issues God wants to deal with first, and would run a mile if all they heard on coming through our doors was that they needed to start living apart? Well, I think we start by loving both couples and being genuinely interested in them as people. But beyond that it is going to take real wisdom to know how to deal with each situation, and more than ever we are going to have to call on the Holy Spirit to help and guide us. We mustn't ever go soft on sin, but must remember that it is God who changes lives and all we can ever do is create the environment where those life changes can take place.

THE LAST WORD

We've only touched here on a host of complicated issues. One of the complexities of a peach community is that we don't just have rules for how we deal with a given person or group of people, but look for the wisdom of God in every situation we face, realising that each one is different and will require different handling. My hope is that in these chapters I'll have at least provoked some further questions, and provided a biblical framework within which to try to think about how to resolve issues as they arise.

I'm going to finish with something Paul wrote to the church in Corinth:

> Or do you not know that wrongdoers will not inherit the kingdom of God? Do not be deceived: Neither the sexually immoral nor idolaters nor adulterers nor men who have sex with men nor thieves nor the greedy nor drunkards nor slanderers nor swindlers will inherit the kingdom of God. And that is what some of you were. But you were washed, you were sanctified, you were justified in the name of the Lord Jesus Christ and by the Spirit of our God.
> (1 Corinthians 6:9–11)

I love that phrase 'And that is what some of you were'. This was a church with many people who were once living lifestyles which placed them way outside the kingdom of God, but in this church they found faith, and not only found faith but experienced changed lives as well. Let's pray that we will be a community which sees the same.

SUGGESTED RESOURCES

No Perfect People Allowed
John Burke

Again John deals in detail with some of the issues we have touched on in this chapter.

Making Love
Gary Chapman
A short but excellent book looking at the difference between having sex and making love.

KEVIN & SARAH

KEVIN & SARAH

Kevin and Sarah were both Christians when they married in 1995 with good jobs and comfortable lifestyles. They have another story though about what lay below the surface. Although they were both active in the church community, Sarah knew that her relationship with God was 'not strong' and in fact it seemed to get worse after she got married. On the surface her role in the church seemed secure but in her last five years there, she withdrew. 'I didn't do anything in the church any more in case anyone found out I didn't like going to church,' she says. 'I had a fear of being found out.' Between the couple things weren't good either. Kevin says, 'I was relatively happy in our marriage – however, in hindsight, I think I had become complacent. I took for granted many things Sarah did for us and did not pay attention to her needs. There were times when I suspected something was not quite right and thought she might be involved with other men. During these times she would act differently but this would only last a short while and wouldn't worry me long term.'

In June 2008, Kevin was made redundant. By Christmas when no work was forthcoming the loss began to bite. In the New Year, to help lift Kevin's spirits, Sarah bought him a skiing holiday but whilst he was away, she became the victim of a violent robbery. Kevin says, 'After the horrors of the night Sarah was mugged, she was very different and I knew that something serious was not right.' The event pushed her over the edge and she started an affair with a man who had helped her after the mugging. By spring, Sarah says, 'My head was so messed up I couldn't think straight and leaving Kevin seemed like the best option.' Although they turned to friends within the church for support, people naturally fell into different camps. Sarah says, 'Some people in the church judged me so instead I moved to a new one. I needed to be where people didn't know me and would accept me for who I was at that time.'

Despite his wife leaving the family home, Kevin kept in touch. He says, 'I knew Sarah's actions were caused by something else and that I needed to be there for her. Forgiveness was not a conscious thing.' Although separated, they often met for a meal after work and Sarah gradually came round to the idea of moving back in. The couple turned to Kerith Community Church for practical help on the marriage course. It was a turning point. Sarah says,

'The two people who ran it were un-judging and kind. I felt I couldn't have seen the same people with the same love anywhere else.' Kevin is also a big supporter of the course: 'We had a few very tough weeks at the beginning but as the course progressed and we shared some of our difficulties with the leaders, we shared more with each other and made plans to put into place a number of things we learnt each week. We were gradually learning how to make our relationship stronger. At the end of the course we were hungry for more and so we attended the Alpha course and continued with the marriage course practices.'

In December 2010, Sarah and Kevin renewed their marriage vows. As part of the meeting they shared their story, which was not only brave but exposed some judgemental attitudes from some in the church community. 'Most people loved us anyway, but not everyone knew the full story before we took our vows again, and some have struggled with it. There has been some resistance to us since we were so open about our past and some people are wary of me,' says Sarah.

For Sarah and Kevin God has set them back on the path to a great relationship. They explain, 'The last year has been amazing, better than the first year we were married even. God brought us together and wants us to stay together.'

leadership

Paul and Barnabas appointed elders for them in each church and, with prayer and fasting, committed them to the Lord, in whom they had put their trust.

(Acts 14:23)

If peach communities are to remain peachy, leadership is vital. Without leadership vision becomes fuzzy, people become inward-looking, risks stop being taken and we can start looking more and more like either a coconut or a tomato. If you read the chapter on our history you'll realise that strong leadership, particularly that of Ben Davies over forty-three years as our senior pastor, has been a huge key to our growth as a church. That is true of the past and will be true of our future. It's therefore important to understand what our leadership structure is, and some of the key attributes we look for when identifying new leaders.

ELDERS

As a church we have a team of elders who have ultimate responsibility for all that goes on in the life of the church. The Bible interchangeably uses the terms 'elder' and 'overseer' to describe this group of people. In many ways 'elder' describes the standing these people should have within our community (respected leaders who have a depth of experience and wisdom which is recognised and appreciated by the church) and 'overseer' describes their role in terms of their responsibility for overseeing all that goes on in the church. The responsibility of the elders breaks down into a number of key areas:

Example – One of the most important things elders do is be an example of how to live the Christian life, how to build growing marriages, raise children, do relationships well and handle finances correctly. Also to be open and vulnerable about one's struggles, doubts, fears and weaknesses.

Doctrine - Elders are the ultimate arbiters for interpreting scripture within our community, and for deciding how we apply what the Bible teaches in specific situations. An example would be whether or not we as a church marry divorced people (we usually do).

Culture – As we've already seen, without leadership peaches can quickly drift into being coconuts or tomatoes. The elders are charged with being constantly on the lookout for non-peachy behaviour, and challenging it wherever they see it.

Discipline – Where church discipline is required, elders are the ones who are to bring it, or to make sure it is worked out correctly.

Prayer – The elders are to set the lead in praying in our community. This includes praying together as a team at least twice a month, leading the church-wide prayer meetings, praying for the sick on Sundays.

Direction – The elders set the overall direction of the church. Once a year the elders spend time meeting with the head of every ministry and then have time to seek God for the future direction of the church.

Gatekeepers – Elders are in charge of deciding what comes into the church and what stays outside. That will include being the final arbiters in issues such as who gets to preach from the platform and whom we bring into leadership and on staff.

Empowering – Elders are responsible for ensuring our church is a place where new leaders are constantly being identified and encouraged. There is more on this issue in the next chapter.

Legal – The elders have legal responsibility for all that goes on in the church. They, helped by a couple of people who bring specific legal and financial skills, are the trustees of the limited company which is Kerith Community Church.

Accountability – These responsibilities are all in a framework wherein the elders are mutually accountable to one another. They also seek advice from leaders of other churches with whom they have a relationship, and intentionally build those relationships. As leaders we have benefited over the years from input by outstanding leaders from many strands of churches – there is more on this in chapter 22.

New elders are chosen from amongst the existing leadership where we recognise people with the appropriate character and gifting (see 1 Timothy 3:1–7 and Titus 1:5–9). Usually these people will be fulfilling the roles and requirements of an elder long before we give them the official title. After the elders have identified a potential new elder they will talk to the church, asking for both positive and negative comments on the person, as well as seeking the opinion of one or two respected leaders outside our community. As long as this doesn't unearth anything untoward, we will then on a Sunday formally recognise the person as an elder.

> **As we've grown, the elders have become**
> **less and less involved in the day-to-day running**
> **of the church. This is an inevitable consequence of growth,**
> **as discovered by both Moses[111] and the apostles.[112]**

With growth the role of the elders becomes more and more to define and protect the soil of the church, where others will be able to serve and minister and where God will be able to move. The elders therefore delegate the day-to-day running of the church to a staff team, who under the authority of the elders are responsible for 'making church happen'.

Our belief is that the New Testament norm is for elders to be men. This comes from the practice of the early church, the qualifications for eldership which Paul lays down in 1 Timothy 3 and Titus 1, and our understanding of the teaching of Paul on the roles of men and women in 1 Corinthians 7, 11 and 14 and in 1 Timothy 2. That doesn't mean that there may not be situations where women are elders, just as Deborah was a judge over the nation of Israel,[113] but that isn't going to be the norm.

Having said that, we believe that under the authority of the elders both men and women can hold any position within the church. Both men and women can preach, teach, lead worship, lead ministries, lead small groups and do anything else in the life of our community.

LEADERSHIP QUALITIES

As we grow as a church we are going to need many, many more leaders. In the next chapter we're going to take a look at some of the things we will need to do to in order to empower new leaders, but I want to finish this chapter by looking at some of the characteristics we look for in those up and coming leaders.

In Acts 6 we read of a time when the early church needed to find a whole new group of leaders:

> Now in these days when the disciples were increasing in number, a complaint by the Hellenists arose against the Hebrews because their widows were being neglected in the daily distribution. And the twelve summoned the full number of the disciples and said:
>
> 'It is not right that we should give up preaching the word of God to serve tables. Therefore, brothers, pick out from among you seven men of good repute, full of the Spirit and of wisdom, whom we will appoint to this duty. But we will devote ourselves to prayer and to the ministry of the word.'
>
> And what they said pleased the whole gathering, and they chose Stephen, a man full of faith and of the Holy Spirit, and Philip, and Prochorus, and Nicanor, and Timon, and Parmenas, and Nicolaus, a proselyte of Antioch. These they set before the apostles, and they prayed and laid their hands on them. (Acts 6:1–6, ESV)

Let's look at some of the things they looked for in these emerging leaders:

Of good repute

As the apostles looked to appoint new leaders they looked for people who were already established and respected within the community, rather than looking for people who were new or were going to come in from outside.

There are huge advantages to raising leaders from within. First of all you have a much clearer idea of what you are going to get. A person's gifting may be very obvious, but their true character can take a lot longer to be revealed. That's really important as we always want to place character above gifting. Secondly, if people have already earned the respect of the community through their willingness to serve and the way they treat others, it will be much easier for those people to step into positions of leadership and influence as opposed to someone new coming in from outside.

Full of the Spirit

Being full of the Spirit doesn't necessarily mean going round performing all sorts of amazing miracles – not many of us would be leaders if that were a requirement! It was certainly true that both Stephen and Philip out of the seven went on to do that sort of thing, but we see from the life of Jesus that there is a difference between being full of the Holy Spirit[114] and moving in the power of the Holy Spirit.[115] What we want are people who are growing in the fruit of the Holy Spirit, displaying growing amounts of love, joy, peace, patience, kindness, goodness, faithfulness, gentleness and self-control.[116]

Full of wisdom

There is a big difference between knowledge and wisdom. Knowledge is knowing information; wisdom is knowing God. It isn't enough even to have lots of knowledge about God and know the Bible back to front. We want leaders who know God, who are passionate about him, who have a growing relationship with him, who are on an adventure with him.

Knowing God also means having leaders who find their identity in God, not in their leadership position. Often the maturity of a person is demonstrated not when they are asked to lead but when they are asked to step down or do something different. How many times have I seen all the toys come out of the pram at that moment! Our identity must be in our adoption as sons and daughters of God, not in our leadership role or title.

Full of faith

The apostles wanted these new leaders to be free thinkers and risk takers. They might have started out waiting on tables but they were going to end up taking huge faith risks, and in Stephen's case being stoned to death for the risk he took.

Leaders are people who take risks, who take the thing they're leading in new directions and to places it hasn't been before. Managers are people who take what they have and keep it going; leaders are those who take what they don't have and make new things happen. We need managers who can maintain and sustain ministries, but we also need leaders who will cause us to do things we've never done before. That often means leading with uncertainty. A lot of the time we won't have all the answers, or a guarantee that what we are doing is going to succeed. I love the attitude of Jonathan when he says to his armour bearer, 'Come, let's go over to the outpost of those uncircumcised men. Perhaps the LORD will act in our behalf.' [117] We need leaders who will go on the strength of a 'perhaps'.

Risk taking means having what some call a 'theology of failure', an understanding that if something doesn't work we're not to bury our heads in the sand and spend months seeking God for what went wrong, but to pick ourselves up, learn from the experience and then move on to the next risk. Failure in our culture is not an option, it is a necessity, and if we aren't doing some things which fail we probably aren't taking enough risks. Risk taking also means taking risks with others, being willing to entrust leadership to people who are different from us or who may not yet have it all sorted. More of this in the next chapter on empowerment.

Courageous Leadership
Bill Hybels

If I had to recommend one book on leadership it would be this one. Bill is perhaps the most inspiring leader I have ever had the privilege of listening to and observing.

SUGGESTED RESOURCES

Humilitas
John Dickson

Analyses the place of humility in achieving true greatness.

Axiom
Bill Hybels

A collection of the leadership principles by which Bill Hybels leads.

The Global Leadership Summit

An annual leadership gathering which takes place in Willow Creek Community Church in Chicago every August, and is then shown around the world over the following months via DVD.

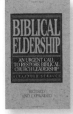

Biblical Eldership
Alexander Strauch

This excellent exposition on the role and requirements of an elder is the best thing I have ever read on the subject.

empowerment

When he came to Jerusalem, he tried to join the disciples, but they were all afraid of him, not believing that he really was a disciple. But Barnabas took him and brought him to the apostles. He told them how Saul on his journey had seen the Lord and that the Lord had spoken to him, and how in Damascus he had preached fearlessly in the name of Jesus.

(Acts 9:26–27)

One of the key responsibilities of leaders is to do themselves out of a job, to raise up the next generation and, in time, to hand over the leadership of their ministry and ultimately the church to them. We are committed to raising up and empowering the next generation. To seeing the knowledge and wisdom of the old combined with the passion and energy of the young in order to see the next generation raised up and the church continue to thrive.

BARNABAS

One of my favourite, and I believe one of the most overlooked, figures in the story of the early church is Barnabas. He was known as the son of encouragement, rose to prominence because of his financial giving, and gives us a great model for the ingredients we need to develop a culture of empowerment. Let's take a look at those ingredients.

EMPOWERMENT – FIRST CHANCES

One of the most powerful examples of encouragement in the life of Barnabas comes not long after Saul (later to be Paul) has met with Jesus and become a Christian on the road to Damascus. Saul begins preaching in Damascus, but after a while the opposition there gets too strong and he leaves and travels to Jerusalem so that he can spend time with the disciples there. When Saul comes to Jerusalem, he tries to join the disciples, but not surprisingly they are suspicious of his conversion story and fear that he is really a spy still intent on getting them all thrown in jail.[118]

But Barnabas takes him and brings him to the apostles. He tells them how Saul on his journey had seen the Lord and that the Lord had spoken to him, and how in Damascus he had preached fearlessly in the name of Jesus. So Saul stays with them and moves about freely in Jerusalem, speaking boldly in the name of the Lord.

> **I love what Barnabas does here.**

First of all he takes a huge personal risk and reaches out to Saul. He doesn't just write him off out of hand, but goes to him and hears his story, and clearly in hearing that story is convinced that he is the real deal, that his conversion is genuine. (He may also have heard independent reports from Damascus.) This could have gone horribly wrong for Barnabas. He could have ended up in jail or even lost his own life, but he was willing to take a risk with Saul for the sake of the gospel.

Then he puts his own reputation on the line by speaking to the apostles on behalf of Saul. He uses his own personal favour with the apostles to speak up for Saul.

Then finally in Acts 11 we read how Barnabas brings Saul under his ministry wing and they begin to work together in Antioch.[119]

I believe that God is going to bring lots of Sauls to us as a community. Maybe not people with quite his history or reputation, but people who 'have a past', and maybe wouldn't fit immediately into our culture or way of thinking, and whom we wouldn't naturally think of using in ministry or leadership positions. Or people who are 'too young', 'too old', 'not clever enough' or for whatever reason don't fit into our leadership mould. What those people are going to need is a Barnabas in their world. Someone who will take a chance with them, who will believe in them, be willing to stand alongside them as they come into the life of our community and then help them to be effective in an area of ministry. Not necessarily an elder or senior leader, but just someone like Barnabas who is respected in our community and willing to take a risk.

Many of us will remember Ed Garton, who was part of our church and sadly passed away in 2010. Ed was a fabulous guy, but he also had a past; he was one of life's rough diamonds. One of Ed's favourite stories was how not long after he became a Christian and came to the church, he became a head steward with responsibility for counting the offering. Nobody had trusted Ed with that sort of responsibility in years, and he and his family were overwhelmed that people were willing to trust him. Ed went on to have a huge impact in many of our lives, and in Uganda and Serenje, but that was all rooted in a few individuals being willing to get alongside and invest their lives in him early in his time in the church community.

Who is God calling you to believe in and empower in our community?

EMPOWERMENT – SECOND CHANCES

The Bible is full of people getting second chances. To take two examples there is David after he commits adultery with Bathsheba (just take a look at Psalm 51 if you want to know what genuine repentance looks like), and Peter after he denies Christ three times. Both messed up big time, but both went on to be restored and to continue to live powerful lives for God.

Part of Barnabas' gift of encouragement is giving second chances. We see this when he and Paul fall out over Mark (the writer of the gospel of Mark). We read about this in Acts 15:

> Some time later Paul said to Barnabas, 'Let us go back and visit the believers in all the towns where we preached the word of the Lord and see how they are doing.' Barnabas wanted to take John, also called Mark, with them, but Paul did not think it wise to take him, because he had deserted them in Pamphylia and had not continued with them in the work. They had such a sharp disagreement that they parted company. Barnabas took Mark and sailed for Cyprus, but Paul chose Silas and left, commended by the believers to the grace of the Lord. (Acts 15:36–40)

The Bible doesn't comment on whether Paul or Barnabas was right in this situation, but my strong feeling is that Barnabas handled it better than Paul. Barnabas was willing to give a second chance to Mark, whereas Paul (who had been on the end of such a strong 'first chance' encouragement from Barnabas) wasn't willing to extend that same chance to Mark. Imagine how Mark would have felt if they'd both rejected him (would he have even ended up writing his gospel?), and imagine how encouraged he must have felt knowing that Barnabas so believed in him that he was willing to sacrifice his ministry partnership with Paul in order to express that belief in him. The issue here isn't whether or not Mark had messed up – he clearly had – but how people around him looked to restore him to community and to his ministry.

It does seem that later in life Paul comes to see the value of Mark's ministry, and that the two of them are reconciled, when he writes to Timothy 'Get Mark and bring him with you, because he is helpful to me in my ministry.' [120] I love those little details and glimpses of hope we get in the Bible!

Part of our culture of empowerment must be to give people second chances. Whether it is people coming into our community having made mistakes elsewhere, or dealing with people who make mistakes when they are in leadership with us, we need to be extending second chances to people.

EMPOWERMENT – STEPPING ASIDE

I don't know if you've ever noticed it, but where we have pairs of names the order of the names is often important. Normally we put the name of the more important or more significant person first. So for instance we talk about 'Cameron and Clegg', 'Moses and Aaron' and 'Ant and Dec' (OK, that last one doesn't work, but you get the idea!).

This sometimes gives an interesting insight into what is going on. Take the example of a couple called 'Priscilla and Aquila' from the book of Acts. Commentators say that the order of their names is interesting because normally the man's name would be first, so Priscilla being named before her husband suggests that she had the more prominent ministry position within their relationship.

A similar study of Paul and Barnabas is very interesting. Up until Acts 13 it's always been 'Barnabas and Saul' whenever their names go together, and Barnabas seems to take the lead as they minister together. But then in Acts 13 Paul produces a barnstorming sermon (starting at verse 16), and from then on it becomes 'Paul and Barnabas' whenever they are mentioned together. Something changes in the dynamic of their ministry, to such an extent that after they part ways over the question of what to do with Mark, we never hear of Barnabas or his ministry again.

So often people end up getting their worth and their value from what they do, from their ministry, their job title or the platforms they stand on. People like that find it very hard when they end up stepping aside to let others take on their ministry, and even more so when a leader over them asks them to step aside.

In my view one of the greatest marks of maturity of a Christian is not how you respond when someone asks you to start doing something, but how you respond when they ask you to stop! That's so often when people throw all their toys out of the pram, leave churches, wreck relationships and seek to destroy what they've built.

One of the joys for me of leading the church is that Ben Davies has been such a remarkable Barnabas in my life. Many people have commented to me that it is almost unprecedented that Ben, who led the church for forty-three years, can still be a part of the church without us falling out. That is largely down to the Barnabas gift of encouragement God has put into Ben, and his amazing ability to continue to be one of my biggest cheerleaders, supporters, advisors and friends in a season when it might now be 'Simon and Ben' rather than 'Ben and Simon'.

I pray that you and I might have the same spirit that Ben demonstrates. Any of us who are leaders are one day going to have to hand our 'baby' on to someone else, whether we make the decision or someone else makes it for us. Let's choose to handle that like a Barnabas, and not fight the new leader every step of the way.

....

The Starfish and the Spider
Ori Brafman and Rod A. Beckstrom

A fascinating analysis of how organisations like eBay and Wikipedia are establishing a whole new organisational structure which challenges the traditional top-down approach. Part of our empowering the next generation will be building churches which are more 'starfish' and less 'spider' in their leadership structure.

> So Christ himself gave the apostles, the prophets, the evangelists, the pastors and teachers, to equip his people for works of service, so that the body of Christ may be built up until we all reach unity in the faith and in the knowledge of the Son of God and become mature, attaining to the whole measure of the fullness of Christ.

(Ephesians 4:11–13)

One of our strengths as a church over the years has been our connectedness, our links with people who have helped us along the journey and with others whom we have been able to help.

For the first seven years after Ben Davies came to lead the church as its first full-time minister, a proportion of his salary was paid by the Baptist Union, starting with seven tenths in the first year. Without that belief and investment in Ben we'd never be where we are today. The Baptist Union also helped with the 1968 church building by lending money at a low interest rate.

Ben, and through him the church, was then hugely influenced by his being a member of the Westminster Fellowship, which was led by Dr Martyn Lloyd-Jones.

From 1975 onwards the church got a lot of help from Campus Crusade for Christ. In 1978 they sponsored Ben to visit the United States and it was on this trip, whilst in Dallas, that Ben got the vision to build the Kerith Centre. It was also through Campus Crusade for Christ that Ben first met Terry Virgo, and our connection with the Newfrontiers family of churches began. This was at a time when the wider church was rediscovering what came to be known as the Ephesians 4 ministries of apostles and prophets. Ben was a part of the top leadership team of Newfrontiers and had major input into churches both in the UK and in countries such as Germany, Kenya, India, South Africa and Zimbabwe.

SWIMMING IN DIFFERENT POOLS

Newfrontiers continues to be our primary 'family' relationship. I regularly meet with other Newfrontiers leaders, both one on one and in larger gatherings, and there are numerous places where we work alongside other Newfrontiers churches, both in the UK and in places such as the Balkans.

However, one of our strengths over the years has been that we have swum in different pools, and have had an openness to learn from as many other places as we can. We have never been content to limit ourselves to our denomination, or our network, but have always built relationships on a much wider basis.

Willow Creek Community Church in Chicago has been a huge influence on us. Bill Hybels and the team there have taught us so much about leadership, excellence, bigness and building a church with a passion for lost people. We wouldn't be the church we are today without that connection.

I personally have been hugely influenced by meeting up with people like John Burke from Gateway Church in Texas, Erwin McManus from Mosaic Church in LA, and Kong Hee from City Harvest Church in Singapore. Not only have we read these people's books and listened to their podcasts, but we have set money aside to allow us to visit their churches, go to their conferences and invite them to come and speak with us.

Then in the UK we have looked to build relationships with and learn from people who are further on than us. As we look to grow from being a church of 1,000 now, one of the keys has been getting around people who are already leading churches of thousands to learn from them. Connections with people like Steve Tibbert in Catford, Dave Smith in Peterborough and the team at Abundant Life Church in Bradford have helped to shape and form us as a church. Holy Trinity Brompton in London has also helped to shape us through courses such as Alpha and the marriage course.

At the same time we've had the privilege of inputting into others. There was more on this in chapter 15, but suffice to say here that our longing is not only that we be blessed, but that we become a blessing to others too, regardless of what style or flavour of church or organisation they represent.

FINDING OUR OWN FINGERPRINT

There is a danger in all this that we develop a church which doesn't really have its own identity, but is just trying to be a copy of somebody (or everybody) else. I believe that every church is called to have its own fingerprint, its own unique DNA, which will be formed by a combination of the community it is in, the leadership, the people who are in the church and the unique call God has put upon that group of people. Therefore, although we learn and get input from many people, the leaders within our community bear the responsibility of deciding what we take on board, what won't work for us, and how we shape the things we have learnt to work in our particular culture.

RELATIONSHIP, NOT STRUCTURE

I think we are in danger of missing what God did through the rediscovery of the apostolic gifts by thinking it was all about structure and about questions like 'who is your apostle?' and 'whose authority are you under?' Instead I believe we need to rediscover that it was the power of relationships which originally made those apostolic movements so powerful. That we need to discover the power of finding those outside our churches with complementary gifts which can help us to grow personally and grow our churches, rather than just being forced together because we're in the same denomination, in the same area or under the same apostle, despite having little else in common.

GOING FORWARD

To be honest I'm not sure in detail what the future looks like for us. Which connections will wane over the next few years, which will grow stronger and which new ones will start. Who will be the major influences on us and who we will influence. But what I do know is that our future is one of growing connection with and reliance on others. A growing sense not of independence but of interdependence. A growing mutual accountability and desire to learn and grow with others, both in our nation and across the nations.

You'll see the influence of many of the people we have connected with over the years in the books recommended in other chapters. I'd strongly recommend getting hold of anything written by the authors I've referred to in this chapter, or visiting any of the churches mentioned.

SUGGESTED RESOURCES

diversity

Just as a body, though one, has many parts, but all its many parts form one body, so it is with Christ. For we were all baptised by one Spirit so as to form one body—whether Jews or Gentiles, slave or free—and we were all given the one Spirit to drink. Even so the body is not made up of one part but of many.

(1 Corinthians 12:12-14)

God wants us to build a church which truly reflects the community we live in. To be perhaps the only place where people from all the different nations and backgrounds within the community mix. And God wants to build a church where we can express differences, both of theological belief and of style of doing church, without falling out or having to start different churches.

Let me talk briefly about a number of areas where I believe we should see that diversity expressed.

NATIONS

Last time we counted we had people from forty-three different nations in our church community. I personally think that's a huge sign of the favour of God on us as a church, something which the leadership prayed for over a number of years, and something we should never take for granted.

As we saw in chapter 15, we want to be a church that not only reaches the nations but also has the nations amongst us. Paul writes that our identity as part of the kingdom of God trumps any national identity we may have, and so I believe we are called to build churches which cross national divides.

But this must mean more than just having people turning up to church on a Sunday from different nations. We need the nations represented on the platform, on our staff, in our eldership, in our small group leaders and in every other area of church life. This will mean working hard at understanding one another's cultures, identifying what leaders look like in different cultures and working out how we serve people from different cultures well.

ECONOMIC AND EDUCATIONAL DIVERSITY

True diversity means more than just having people from different nations in the church. It is possible to build a church which looks very diverse in terms of different nationalities, but where what you actually have are the middle-class, university-educated professionals from each of those nations. That doesn't represent true diversity.

We want to be a place where millionaires sit next to CAP clients, and they relate to one another as friends rather than one feeling superior to the other. Where professors with PhDs share their lives with people who dropped out of school aged sixteen. Where a single mum on benefits knows she has the same value and worth as the high-flying business woman who is in her Lifegroup. Where the teenager who is studying hairdressing at Bracknell and Wokingham College is as celebrated and applauded as the teenager going to Cambridge to study law.

James speaks powerfully of the attitude we need to have when he writes:

> My brothers and sisters, believers in our glorious Lord Jesus Christ must not show favouritism. Suppose a man comes into your meeting wearing a gold ring and fine clothes, and a poor man in filthy old clothes also comes in. If you show special attention to the man wearing fine clothes and say, 'Here's a good seat for you,' but say to the poor man, 'You stand there' or 'Sit on the floor by my feet,' have you not discriminated among yourselves and become judges with evil thoughts? (James 2:1–4)

AGE DIVERSITY

Another area where we need to strive for diversity is across the ages. We don't want to be just a church for young families, a church for the retired or a youth church. We want to embrace people at every stage of life, and integrate them into everything we do. That means teenagers serving alongside retired people in the kids' work, older people mentoring younger people, people of all ages getting into leadership positions and going on overseas trips.

THEOLOGICAL DIVERSITY

It sometimes makes me laugh (when it's not driving me to despair) to think that many of the groups of Christians who can't get on together here on earth, or who spend their time writing blogs, books and sermons pulling down another group or denomination, are going to end up in heaven together. There aren't going to be multiple areas of heaven, one for the Calvinists, one for the Arminians, one for the people who liked hymns and one for those who preferred choruses. We're all going to be part of one heavenly throng praising one King.

That perspective means that within our community we're going to embrace some theological diversity, some differences in what people might believe on various non-core theological issues.

Take for instance the issue of creation. Some people are convinced that Genesis 1 contains a scientific account of a literal seven-day creation. Others that the language is more poetic, and that the account is more concerned with the question of why things are the way they are than with how scientifically it all happened. People who love Jesus and hold to the authority of the Bible sit on both sides of the fence, and we as a church are not going to take a line on what people should believe.

Or take the question of what exactly is going to happen when Jesus comes again. Is a pre-millennial, post-millennial or amillennial view the correct one to hold? Again we're not going to take a strong line on which view is correct (someone recently told me that they were a pan-millennialist: they believe Jesus is coming again and the rest will just pan out. I like that!).

Now there will be some issues we are crystal clear on and which are non-negotiable. Hopefully by now you've worked out what they are, but they mostly relate to who Jesus was, what his death and resurrection achieved, the authority of the Bible and those sorts of things.

There will be other issues where we take a particular line, such as on the gifts of the Holy Spirit being for today or that baptism is for believers and should be by full immersion in water. We realise other Christians may have a different view, and we'll even have Christians within our church community who hold a different view, but we as a leadership have taken and will teach a particular line.

But there will be other issues, such as the ones I've mentioned here, where we will have a diversity of views.

IN CONCLUSION

It is vital that we realise that we are one church, one body, yet that body has many different parts. We will only truly be the body God wants us to be when we embrace that diversity.

Good to Grow
Steve Tibbert

Steve's story of how the church he leads in south-east London has grown from a few hundred to over 1,000 has much to teach us on many levels, but in particular what he has to say on diversity is incredibly instructive.

Letters Across the Divide
David Anderson and Brent Zuercher

Two friends on opposite sides of the racial divide write a series of letters to each other, exploring each other's view of racism and how it affects them. I might not have explained it well, but this is a deeply moving book and one I would recommend everyone read.

Who Stole My Church?
Gordon MacDonald

In this brilliant book, written as a story about the clash between the younger and older generations in a church, Gordon explores some of what it takes for the different age groups to understand and appreciate one another.

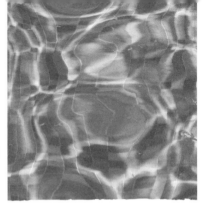

baptism

Peter replied, 'Repent and be baptised, every one of you, in the name of Jesus Christ for the forgiveness of your sins. And you will receive the gift of the Holy Spirit. The promise is for you and your children and for all who are far off—for all whom the Lord our God will call.'

With many other words he warned them; and he pleaded with them, 'Save yourselves from this corrupt generation.' Those who accepted his message were baptised, and about three thousand were added to their number that day.

(Acts 2:38–41)

Our baptism Sundays are one of the most exciting events in our calendar. It's always amazing to hear the stories of how God has moved in people's lives. How people have found hope, freedom, forgiveness, a family, a sense of purpose and meaning in their lives. How people far, far from God have discovered what it means to have a relationship with him.

One of our key goals as a community is to see people saved and added – not just to see people respond to an appeal and pray a prayer, but to see them become fully devoted followers of Jesus Christ and be added to the church community.

For us baptism is a key part in that process as a public declaration and celebration, not only of choosing to follow Christ but also of joining the family of believers. As people move from belonging to believing to behaving it's a public declaration that they've made the step of believing, that they've moved closer to the core.

WHAT IS BAPTISM?

The Greek word for baptism means 'to plunge, dip or immerse something in water'. It is the word used to describe what has happened when a ship sinks, or somebody drowns.

The Bible makes it clear that Jesus was baptised[121] and that he expected people who followed him to be baptised too.[122]

As we read through the book of Acts we see that the early church followed this command to baptise new believers, whether it was in the aftermath of the Holy Spirit falling at Pentecost,[123] people responding to the preaching of Philip,[124] the Ethiopian eunuch coming to faith,[125] Saul after his conversion,[126] Cornelius and his household after they were saved,[127] Lydia and her household,[128] the jailer and his household,[129] Crispus and a bunch of people in Corinth[130] or Paul finding some disciples in Ephesus.[131] In each case baptism is a public declaration of faith in Jesus, and of having joined and identified with the community of the church.

It's important to be clear that baptism is a symbol, an external representation of what God has already done on the inside. Being baptised doesn't make you a Christian, and you don't need to be baptised to be a Christian (the thief on the cross who died next to Jesus was never baptised, but Jesus said he would be with him in paradise). [132]

We also need to be clear that being baptised is something people should undertake after they've believed. On the day of Pentecost we read that 'Those who accepted his message were baptised'.[133] It was those who had already chosen to repent and follow Christ who were baptised. That means that children can be baptised as long as they are old enough to understand what they are doing.

Being totally immersed in water, and then (hopefully) being lifted out again, is primarily a symbol of us identifying with Jesus in his death, burial and resurrection. Paul writes:

> Or don't you know that all of us who were baptised into Christ Jesus were baptised into his death? We were therefore buried with him through baptism into death in order that, just as Christ was raised from the dead through the glory of the Father, we too may live a new life. (Romans 6:3–4)

By getting baptised we're saying that through his death and resurrection we too have died to our old way of life and have risen to a whole new life in him. No wonder our baptisms are such great times of celebration.

Baptism is also sometimes seen as a picture of our sin being washed away. Paul writes to Titus that 'He saved us through the washing of rebirth'.[134] Baptism is also linked with being filled with the Holy Spirit, as Peter indicated on the day of Pentecost: 'Repent and be baptised, every one of you, in the name of Jesus Christ for the forgiveness of your sins. And you will receive the gift of the Holy Spirit.' [135]

WHAT ABOUT YOU?

So have you been baptised? Not as an infant before you came to faith, or with just a sprinkling, but as a believer getting properly drenched!

If not then I'd really encourage you to sign up to be baptised. If you get baptised with us then we'll get you to do a short course, to make sure you understand what you're doing and to help you prepare your personal story. You can then have your own opportunity to publicly declare what Christ has done for you – do it!

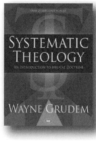

**Systematic Theology
Wayne Grudem**

SUGGESTED RESOURCES

If you want to study baptism in more detail I'd suggest investing in a copy of this book. If you haven't come across a systematic theology before, it is a book which takes a range of different subjects and for each one of them looks at what the whole of the Bible has to say on that subject. I'd recommend that everyone buy one!

communion

> **They devoted themselves to the apostles' teaching and to fellowship, to the breaking of bread and to prayer.**

(Acts 2:42)

In the last chapter we looked at baptism. Baptism is something done once, as a sign of someone beginning their Christian life. In contrast communion, or the Lord's supper as it is sometimes known, is something which is to be done regularly as a sign of our ongoing relationship with Jesus.

We first read of communion in the New Testament when Jesus takes it with his disciples.

> While they were eating, Jesus took bread, and when he had given thanks, he broke it and gave it to his disciples, saying, 'Take and eat; this is my body.' Then he took a cup, and when he had given thanks, he gave it to them, saying, 'Drink from it, all of you. This is my blood of the covenant, which is poured out for many for the forgiveness of sins. I tell you, I will not drink from this fruit of the vine from now on until that day when I drink it new with you in my Father's kingdom.' (Matthew 26:26–29)

The early church continued this pattern:

> Every day they continued to meet together in the temple courts. They broke bread in their homes and ate together with glad and sincere hearts, praising God and enjoying the favour of all the people. (Acts 2:46–47)

The phrase 'breaking bread' refers to them having communion in their homes as part of sharing a meal together, telling us something about the context in which they took communion.

147

SO WHAT IS COMMUNION?

Communion is believers coming together to eat bread and drink wine (or grape juice). It is clear from what Paul wrote to the church in Corinth that this was something Jesus expected us to do to remember him:

> For I received from the Lord what I also passed on to you: The Lord Jesus, on the night he was betrayed, took bread, and when he had given thanks, he broke it and said, 'This is my body, which is for you; do this in remembrance of me.' In the same way, after supper he took the cup, saying, 'This cup is the new covenant in my blood; do this, whenever you drink it, in remembrance of me.' For whenever you eat this bread and drink this cup, you proclaim the Lord's death until he comes. (1 Corinthians 11:23–26)

In taking communion we not only remember Jesus' life, death and resurrection, but we also look forward to the time when we will eat it again with him in heaven at what the Bible calls the wedding supper of the Lamb.[136]

Communion also makes a powerful statement about our unity together as a family of Christians, as we at least symbolically all share from one loaf:

> Is not the cup of thanksgiving for which we give thanks a participation in the blood of Christ? And is not the bread that we break a participation in the body of Christ? Because there is one loaf, we, who are many, are one body, for we all share the one loaf. (1 Corinthians 10:16–17)

HOW SHOULD WE DO COMMUNION?

First of all we need to be clear that communion is for believers, for those who have already crossed the line of faith and chosen to follow Jesus. This means that whenever we have communion in a context where unbelievers are present we will be careful to explain that this is for believers only, and encourage unbelievers not to take it. We will also seek to do it in a way which doesn't mark unbelievers out or make them feel excluded or unwelcome. Hopefully we will be clear enough about the gospel on a regular basis for people to know on which side of that line of faith they sit.

Because of this sensitivity to unbelievers, we have tended over the last few years to have communion in settings such as Lifegroups and prayer meetings where we don't have to explain all of this. However, that doesn't have to be the case if we explain it well.

Before taking communion we should examine our hearts to make sure that we are in right relationship with God and with one another. Paul writes to the church in Corinth, where communion is highlighting divisions between the rich and the poor – in the light of the chapter on justice, chapter 14, I find it fascinating that it is the treatment of the poor which causes Paul to question how they are doing communion. Paul is pretty clear when he writes:

> Everyone ought to examine themselves before they eat of the bread and drink from the cup. For those who eat and drink without discerning the body of Christ eat and drink judgment on themselves. That is why many among you are weak and sick, and a number of you have fallen asleep. (1 Corinthians 11:28–30)

The way we take communion will be a reflection of how we see Christ and whether he is truly Lord of our lives, so it shouldn't be a surprise that God takes a wrong attitude to communion very seriously. Not because he is passionate about communion as such, but because he is passionate about his Son.

The Bible doesn't say anything about who should be in charge of taking communion, or give us any specific instructions about how often or in what gatherings it should be taken. In the early church it does however seem to have been taken fairly regularly, even daily, and in a context which was small enough for them to have a meal together and to use a single loaf.

WHERE DOES THIS FIT FOR US?

It is clear that communion was a central part of the life of the early church. Somehow that regular reconnection with Christ and recognition of who they were in him was incredibly important and powerful for them.

Yet it seems for us that we don't really know what to do with communion. Whichever context we do it in, it often seems like we're just doing it because we're supposed to. Somewhere along the line it feels like we've missed its true significance and power. As I've travelled around the world and visited many different churches, it has seemed that often it is the 'traditional' churches which give communion the most significance and where I've had the most powerful encounters with God, and it is in taking it with a few friends in a home setting where I have most connected with the sense of doing it as a body. I still think there is something huge for us to rediscover with communion; it's going to be an exciting journey as we do.

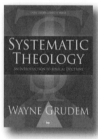

Systematic Theology
Wayne Grudem
As with baptism I'd suggest this if you want to study communion in more detail.

spirit filled

In the last days, God says, I will pour out my Spirit on all people. Your sons and daughters will prophesy, your young men will see visions, your old men will dream dreams. Even on my servants, both men and women, I will pour out my Spirit in those days, and they will prophesy.

(Acts 2:17–18)

One of the strangest things Jesus ever said was that it was for our benefit that he was going to go into heaven and would not be with us any more.[137] That seems like a pretty weird claim. Surely the best thing we could ever have would be still to have Jesus with us; that was certainly how it seemed to the disciples. But he was very clear that it was for our good that he was going away, because when he got to heaven he was going to send the Holy Spirit, so that rather than just having God among us we could have God living in each one of us.

Then fifty days after Jesus ascends into heaven, on what the Jews called the day of Pentecost, this amazing thing happens: the Holy Spirit is poured out on a little band of believers and they immediately spill out onto the streets and in a day see their fledgling church go from being a fairly manageable community of 120 to being a megachurch of over 3,000.[138]

One of the most remarkable aspects of this outpouring is that the Holy Spirit is poured out on everyone.

Not just a few special people for a limited period of time to do a particular job, as had happened in the Old Testament (Bezalel,[139] Samson,[140] Gideon[141]), but on men and women, young people and old people, everyone. Suddenly people didn't have to go through a priest to get to God but everyone became a priest.[142] Everyone had this direct access to God because everyone now had God's Spirit living within them.

Jesus clearly saw the work of the Holy Spirit as being key to our living out the life God has called us to. But often Christians are fuzzy and vague about the Holy Spirit and what part he has to play in our lives today. As part of the core of the peach we want to be very clear about these things, so here goes!

TRINITY

Although the Bible never uses the word 'trinity' it is very clear that God is a trinity, one God but three persons: God the Father, God the Son and God the Holy Spirit. The Bible is very clear that each of them is fully God (see for example John 1:1 explicitly saying Jesus was God) but that there is only God. Now that is a mystery! Anyone who claims to be able to understand or explain how that works is mistaken or deluded, and any picture you may have been given to explain it (water in its various states, the different bits of an egg, the same person being a father, a husband and a son and numerous others) is inadequate and probably heretical!

God is so far beyond our comprehension and understanding, his ways and thoughts are so much higher than ours, that none of this should surprise us or worry us. The trinity shouldn't leave us confused, or worried that we can't put God in a box and explain him, but lead us to worship God with a fresh sense of his majesty and wonder.

THE HOLY SPIRIT

We first encounter the Holy Spirit in Genesis 1 when he (not 'it'; the Holy Spirit is a person, not an object) is hovering over creation, bringing order out of the chaos. We encounter him again as he comes on various Old Testament characters to do particular jobs. But all the way through the Old Testament is a promise that a new day is coming when the Holy Spirit will be poured out on everyone. A day when the Holy Spirit will totally transform the way we relate to God by giving us a heart transplant, by taking our hearts of stone and giving us hearts of flesh. A day is coming when we will no longer relate to God by trying externally to keep the law, but instead God's law will be written on our hearts and we will obey him by the power of the Holy Spirit living within us.

And then we see the Holy Spirit powerfully at work in the life of Jesus. He is conceived of the Holy Spirit,[143] John the Baptist is filled with the Holy Spirit before he is born,[144] at his baptism the Holy Spirit comes on Jesus like a dove.[145] Jesus then goes out to the desert to be tempted full of the Holy Spirit,[146] and returns from the desert in the power of the Holy Spirit.[147] Everything he does is through the Holy Spirit, and all through his life he is promising a new era of the Holy Spirit.

Then on the day of Pentecost this all comes to fruition as the Holy Spirit is poured out on all the believers.[148]

But it doesn't stop there. This experience of being filled with the Holy Spirit is seen to be a repeatable one.

Repeatable for those who were filled on the day of Pentecost, but also repeatable in the lives of those converted after Pentecost. We see this when Cornelius and his household are saved.[149] In fact the evidence for Peter that God has truly accepted these Gentile believers into the kingdom of God is that they 'received the Holy Spirit just as we did'.[150]

We see it when Saul is converted on the road to Damascus and Ananias comes to him and lays hands on him for him to be filled with the Holy Spirit.[151] We see it when Paul turns up in Ephesus and asks the believers there whether they have received the Holy Spirit.[152] Sometimes this experience of being filled with the Holy Spirit happens at the point of conversion, sometimes there is a gap between the two events; there doesn't seem to be a clear pattern. But what is clear is that people knew that they had been filled with the Holy Spirit. This wasn't just some theoretical idea; it was an experience which allowed Paul to ask in Ephesus 'did you receive the Holy Spirit when you believed?'[153]

CAN THIS BE PEACHY?

My observation is that some people seeking to build 'peachy' churches go quiet when it comes to the idea of praying for people to be filled with the Holy Spirit, or using the gifts of the Holy Spirit such as prophecy or tongues (I heard someone jokingly describe churches like this as 'non-prophet organisations'). They become worried that all this Holy Spirit activity might appear weird or off-putting to people far from God.

I don't believe that it has to be like that. In fact by factoring out the work of the Holy Spirit we're in danger of robbing all these lost and broken people coming into our peachy communities of the power of the Holy Spirit which can truly transform them. Take the example of Alpha.

ALPHA

One of the most powerful evangelistic tools of the last couple of decades has been the Alpha Course. In the middle of the Alpha Course is a day or a weekend away where the whole focus is on explaining all about the work of the Holy Spirit, and then praying for people to experience the power of the Holy Spirit. I remember the first Alpha day away I ever led, and in particular two guys who were on that course. One was an avowed sceptic who had only come on the course because of constant requests from his wife. The other was an ex-army guy who was as tough as nails and sat at the back showing no interest in what was happening.

At the end of the session on being filled with the Holy Spirit I asked people forward and we started to pray for them. God met powerfully with a number of people, but these two guys just sat in their seats.

After a while I summoned up the courage to ask them individually what was happening, and to my amazement both told me that they were having incredibly powerful encounters with God, one even saying that he was having to hold on to the seat because he didn't know what would happen if he let go.

I don't know what you make of that. I'm not sure myself what my theology is on praying for people who aren't yet Christians to be filled with the Holy Spirit. But what I do know is that that day God changed the lives of those two men, such that they have never been the same since. What we had failed to do through hours of talks, relationship building and answering questions, God did in a moment in each of them.

I believe that part of the genius of Alpha is that it creates a safe environment for people far from God to experience the power of God. I believe that it is the same environment, the same soil, which we need to create in order for God to do all that he wants to do amongst us.

WHAT ABOUT YOU?

In the next chapter we'll wrestle with what it means to create space for the Holy Spirit to move in a way which doesn't confuse or put off lost people, but allows them to experience the power of God in a life-changing way. But as we finish this chapter I want to throw a personal challenge out to you, regarding where you might be in terms of all we've talked about in this chapter. I'd like to ask you a few questions, if that's OK.

Perhaps you've never experienced being filled with the Holy Spirit? Let me be clear that this doesn't make you in any sense a 'second-class' Christian, but it does mean that you're not living with all of God's power which is available to you. If you've never had a powerful encounter with God, if your relationship with God is a thing of the head rather than a thing of the heart, then I'd encourage you to start seeking God to be filled with the Holy Spirit. I'd start by reading the book of Acts and noting each occasion where someone is filled with the Spirit, and then finding a group of people to pray for you to be filled. I had a gap of a year between first asking God to fill me with the Holy Spirit and actually being filled, so keep asking.[154]

Secondly, if you have been filled then are you growing in the fruit of the Spirit? [155] Being filled with the Spirit is no guarantee of or short cut to spiritual maturity. Some of the most immature Christians I've ever met were those who claimed to be most full of the Spirit. And Paul reminds us that all the gifts of the Spirit are a total waste of time if not worked out with a heart of love.[156]

And then finally how actively are you seeking spiritual gifts?[157] The New Testament identifies a whole range of spiritual gifts which we should actively be seeking to grow in.

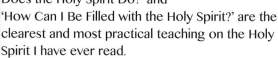

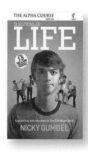

Questions of Life
Nicky Gumbel
The chapters in this book on 'Who Is the Holy Spirit?', 'What Does the Holy Spirit Do?' and 'How Can I Be Filled with the Holy Spirit?' are the clearest and most practical teaching on the Holy Spirit I have ever read.

SUGGESTED
RESOURCES

Joy Unspeakable
D. Martyn Lloyd-Jones
This is not the easiest read in the world, but if you want an in-depth analysis of what the Bible teaches on being filled with the Holy Spirit you can't do better than this.

spirit filled peaches

So if the whole church comes together and everyone speaks in tongues, and enquirers or unbelievers come in, will they not say that you are out of your mind?

(1 Corinthians 14:23)

We believe in the importance of being filled with the Holy Spirit, and in the gifts of the Holy Spirit for today. Yet at the same time we are committed to building a church where unchurched people can come and feel that this is a safe place for them to be. Where they aren't going to be put off by a bunch of Christians doing things that leave them feeling uncomfortable and confused. As Bill Hybels puts it, where they can find a safe place to hear the dangerous, life-changing message of the gospel.

For those of you for whom Kerith is the only church you've ever been in, what we do on a Sunday and in small groups will seem perfectly normal. Hopefully this chapter will just give you a better idea of why we do what we do.

But some of you reading this will be coming from churches that did things differently from Kerith and will want to know whether this is a place where you can 'fit'. Some of you will be from churches which had an open microphone on a Sunday, where anyone could come and speak if they felt God was giving them something to say. Others will be totally new to all this teaching on being filled with the Holy Spirit and may even disagree with it, and you may want to know whether you'll be welcome here. Hopefully this chapter will help to answer those questions.

BEING PEACHY

The apostle Paul was passionate about the outworking of the Holy Spirit. He boasted to the church in Corinth that he spoke in tongues more than any of them,[158] and wrote to the church in Thessalonica that they shouldn't treat prophecy with contempt but should actively look for it and encourage it.[159]

Yet he was also a man who lived with a passion for the unbeliever, seeking to reach lost people everywhere he went.

In 1 Corinthians chapters 12, 13 and 14 Paul writes in detail about the use of the gifts of the Holy Spirit in a church context. Towards the end of chapter 14 he starts to wrestle with what happens when there are unbelievers in a meeting where the gifts of the Holy Spirit are being used. He writes:

> Tongues, then, are a sign, not for believers but for unbelievers; prophecy, however, is not for unbelievers but for believers. So if the whole church comes together and everyone speaks in tongues, and enquirers or unbelievers come in, will they not say that you are out of your mind?
>
> But if an unbeliever or an enquirer comes in while everyone is prophesying, they are convicted of sin and are brought under judgement by all, as the secrets of their hearts are laid bare. So they will fall down and worship God, exclaiming, 'God is really among you!' (1 Corinthians 14:22–25)

Paul isn't arguing that we should hide spiritual gifts from unbelievers. Quite the opposite, in fact. He points out the incredible impact prophecy can have in the life of the unbeliever as God speaks into the secrets of their hearts, speaks into their pain, their hurt, their guilt, their shame and their broken dreams.

In recent times we've seen a great increase in the number of people who, when they get baptised, refer to a specific prophecy as being a significant part of their journey to faith. We want more of that, not less. But Paul also argues that there are some expressions of spiritual gifts which can be a negative sign for an unbeliever – pointing them not towards faith but away from it. The ESV Study Bible puts it like this:

> 'uninterpreted tongues function as a sign of judgement for the outsider and unbeliever because they may conclude from hearing them that Christians are out of their minds and so leave the church, never to return'. [160]

So, as we look to build a peachy community, what does that look like when it comes to the gifts of the Holy Spirit?

SUNDAYS

Being peachy means that our Sunday meetings, which are our main shop window to the world, are going to be planned. We aren't just going to ask the worship leader to start with a song and then 'see where the Spirit leads'. There will be other contexts and meetings where we do exactly that, but not on a Sunday. So what implications does that have?

We'll have a plan as to what is going to be happening throughout the meeting. That doesn't mean we've planned God out of the meeting; it just means that we believe God can guide us and lead us in our planning as much as he can in a spontaneous contribution on a Sunday. And if the meeting goes as we've planned it, then that doesn't mean that God didn't show up; it hopefully means God was with us in our planning. The reality is that being planned actually gives us a lot more flexibility as we're not just relying on the spontaneous to cover our lack of a plan.

Our Sunday meetings are not going to have an open microphone where anyone can just come and bring a contribution. If somebody feels like they have a contribution to bring, then they'll first need to talk to the site pastor (the leader in charge of the meeting, who usually won't be the preacher), who will make a decision as to what happens. Sometimes they'll run with the contribution, sometimes they might decide it fits better at some other point in the meeting and sometimes they'll say no. If you come with a contribution which doesn't get used then please have a good attitude about it. Perhaps God was speaking to you personally rather than to the whole church, perhaps you didn't quite hear properly from God or perhaps the site pastor got it wrong. Whichever it is, let the site pastor take responsibility for whether it gets used publicly.

In reality most contributions on a Sunday will come from a handful of people with known gifting, and are most likely to come from the preacher or other people already on the platform. Some will ask how we can do this in the light of what Paul has to say in 1 Corinthians 14:

> What then shall we say, brothers and sisters? When you come together, each of you has a hymn, or a word of instruction, a revelation, a tongue or an interpretation. Everything must be done so that the church may be built up. (1 Corinthians 14:26)

I don't believe Paul ever imagined this being worked out in the context of a meeting with several hundred people in it, in a building with a balcony as we have, and where 'each of you' having an opportunity to speak could take several hours. Again there will be contexts where this will be done, but not on a Sunday.

Also, following Paul's directive we won't encourage people to speak in tongues on a Sunday, either from the platform or in the congregation.

We'll also seek to explain everything which happens in the meeting, whether that's taking up the offering, unpacking a prophetic word, praying for the sick or making an appeal. We'll be very clear when asking for any sort of response that nobody is being put under pressure to join in; they are just being given an opportunity to respond to whatever God may be doing. We'll also be very clear about what is going to happen to people if they respond.

Finally, we'll be pretty strict on time. Sunday meetings will start on time (usually with a countdown) and will generally finish on time too. I've been to too many churches where at the time the meeting was supposed to start people were still setting out chairs and the musicians were still practising. That's not being spiritual or spontaneous, it's just being lazy. If we say that a meeting starts at 11.00am then our experience is that unbelievers will get there before it starts (even if none of the Christians do) and expect it to start and finish on time.

If a meeting is going to go more than a couple of minutes beyond the normal end time then we're very open to that. However, at the time the meeting was planned to finish we'll ask people with children to go and pick them up so we serve our children's workers well. And we'll make it clear that although the meeting is going to carry on, people are free to go (guilt free) if they need to.

BELIEVERS' MEETINGS

When we meet together as believers, whether it's in a prayer meeting, a Lifegroup or any other sort of gathering where there are only Christians present, then we can run the meeting very differently. When I meet with the elders I expect 'each of them' to bring their contribution, speak out what God has put on their heart, bring tongues with interpretations and the rest, without me having to stop and explain what is happening.

But we still need to be aware of who is with us. If a non-believer comes to your Lifegroup then you don't just plough on as if they weren't there, but you're aware of their being there and treat them as treasure in your midst.

CONCLUSION

We believe in the gifts of the Holy Spirit, but we also believe that God wants us to be very aware of their impact on lost people in our meetings. If used wrongly then the gifts can turn lost people away from God, but if used correctly then they can be a powerful way for God to speak into their lives.

....

Surprised by the Voice of God
Jack Deere

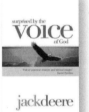

This is a brilliant examination of the ways in which God speaks to us today with some inspirational stories from church history. It also goes into some of the issues we've covered in this chapter.

wolves

Watch out for false prophets. They come to you in sheep's clothing, but inwardly they are ferocious wolves. By their fruit you will recognise them.

(Matthew 7:15–16)

Jesus is very clear that when God begins to move, people will come who will try to mess up God's work. Jesus describes these people as wolves who, although they will appear to be spiritual and full of God on the outside, inwardly will be bent on spoiling what God is doing.

Jesus particularly links wolves with false prophets, which is interesting as usually the way they operate is by wanting to speak into people's lives. That may come through wanting to speak prophetically to people or to give them strong directional advice, or through prayer, which will frequently leave people feeling confused or down. Often these people claim to have an incredible ability to hear from God, and they can even leave us feeling quite inadequate with what seems like their hotline to God. But not everyone who comes to us with an apparently powerful ministry and ability to hear from God will be from God. And all of us have a responsibility to make sure the church is a safe place for lost and broken people to come to, and for the gifts of the Holy Spirit to operate.

Wolves can come to any church, but they can be a particular problem for churches seeking to be peachy because of our desire to be welcoming and open to all sorts of people. That makes it particularly important that everyone in a peachy church is equipped to spot and deal with wolves.

So how do we prevent wolves from wreaking havoc? Well, we need to get good at spotting wolves, and then when we've spotted them we must deal with them.

SPOTTING WOLVES

All of us need to be on the lookout for wolves. There are too many people in our community for the elders or senior leaders to be able to see what goes on in every group. So imagine the scenario: you're in a church meeting, whether on a Sunday or in a small group, and you see somebody deep in conversation and prayer with another person whom you know. You're not sure why, but you don't feel entirely happy with what is going on. What do you do?

Well, first of all, if you're a part of our community it's your responsibility to do something. If there's a leader around then go and check it out with them, at which point it becomes their responsibility. If not, then you need to summon up your courage, be brave, pray, and then go and check out what is going on by breaking into the prayer or conversation between the two people.

So how do you tell whether the person is a wolf? Jesus tells us that we will spot false prophets by their fruit. That fruit displays itself in a number of ways.

First of all, wolves can be known by the fruit of their lives. Are they displaying the fruit of the Holy Spirit?[161] People who come and are critical, aggressive, boastful or proud should be suspected. If they're not part of our church community, are they in another church where they're in good relationship with and submitted to the leadership there, or are they loners going from church to church with little or no accountability?

Secondly, what is the fruit of their ministry? Wolves often want to minister to people alone, in a corner. Often the people they want to minister to will be vulnerable or people on the fringes of our community (wolves rarely attack the strong). This is the total opposite to the spirit of openness we want to see in all of our ministries.

Wolves will also often be unhappy about their ministry being weighed and tested by others. I've had people come to me in the past with prophetic words who have become aggressive when I've questioned whether God has really spoken through them, and have told me that they always hear completely accurately from God and that there is no need for their word to be weighed. I want to be clear that this is completely unbiblical, and should be a strong indication that a wolf is in our midst.

Paul teaches us to weigh all prophecy carefully,[162] because he knows that we only 'know in part, and prophesy in part'.[163] Personally I think one of the most dangerous phrases Christians ever use is 'God told me...' That can so easily be used as the trump card to do whatever we want without anyone being able to question it.

People who really hear from God are always open to having what they say weighed. So if people aren't willing to have what they say weighed by others, or want to take people off to one side to speak to them on their own, we should be very suspicious.

Finally, wolves sometimes come with a very strong opinion on some non-core aspect of what the Bible teaches. I've met people with incredibly strong views on things like what is going to happen when Jesus comes again, the future of Israel as a nation, whether the King James is the only legitimate English Bible translation, the place of deliverance in the life of the believer or Genesis describing a literal seven-day creation. As we saw in chapter 23, we're very comfortable with people in our community having a variety of different views on those things. But when they become non-negotiable, when people start talking about those things more than they talk about Christ, or when they start gathering groups of people together focussed around that one issue, alarm bells should start to ring.

DEALING WITH WOLVES

Hopefully having stepped in you'll have found that nothing untoward was going on. You might even feel slightly embarrassed at having broken into the conversation – please don't. I'm happy for us to have ninety-nine false alarms if it helps us prevent one wolf from doing damage.

But if having stepped in you're still not happy about the situation, what do you do?

First I'd encourage you to stay in the conversation between the two people until it is over. If the person still wants to prophesy, pray or give advice, ask them to do it with you there so that you can hear and weigh what is being said. If you're not happy with what is being said then you have permission to ask them to stop. What they're doing may be entirely appropriate in the community they come from, but that doesn't mean it's acceptable in ours, and if they're truly godly then they'll fully understand where you are coming from.

Secondly, once you're on your own with the person on the receiving end of the conversation, check that they're OK.

Then afterwards speak to a leader, even if that means a phone call after the meeting. Tell them what you've observed. You'll often feel vulnerable at this point and may need them to encourage you and pray for you. They should then follow up on what has happened.

YOU CAN'T BE SERIOUS!

Some of you may think this all sounds very heavy. Well, in the middle of all our talk of peachiness we need to realise that we have an enemy, the devil, who is intent on destroying what God is doing amongst us. One of the ways he will do that is by sending wolves.

Personally I've heard of too many people whose lives have been wrecked by a prophetic word or some strong suggestions or advice which haven't been properly weighed. Part of our responsibility is to make sure that it doesn't happen again.

Little Red Riding Hood
In the absence of anything more theologically satisfying, this story at least shows the importance of identifying and dealing with wolves!

SUGGESTED RESOURCES

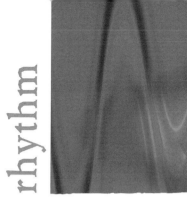

rhythm

Come to me, all you who are weary and burdened, and I will give you rest.

(Matthew 11:28)

There is a danger that a church can become defined simply by all the activity which is going on. Action-packed Sundays, courses, small groups, prayer meetings, conferences, involvement in the community, people travelling around the UK and overseas – all of it undoubtedly good. But if we are just defined by our activity then we can end up with lots of burnt out, emotionally, spiritually and physically exhausted people. Not really what Jesus had in mind when he said that his yoke was easy and his burden was light.

The more I look at the world, and read what the Bible has to say about it, and in particular God's directions to the nation of Israel, the more I realise that God designed the world to have a sense of rhythm.

There was a rhythm as God created. Not only did God stop after six days and take a day's rest (not because he was exhausted and needed a rest but simply because he chose to), but even through the first six days there were moments when God stopped, looked back on all he had already achieved and declared 'it is good'.

THE DAY ➔ There was a rhythm to the day, as God created it with light and dark, day and night. I was much struck the first time I went to rural Zambia, where there was no electricity or artificial lighting, by the fact that when it got dark everybody simply had to stop. One of the impacts of technology has been that we can now work twenty-four hours a day if we want to. Electric lighting means we can now work even when it is dark. Smart phones mean we can be answering email from the moment we wake up to the moment we go to sleep, and when we leave the office many of us just carry on working. We've lost the rhythm of the day. Even meals, which were traditionally times when people stopped, relaxed and connected with others, are taken on the move or on our own.

THE WEEK ➲ There was a rhythm to the week, enshrined in the idea of Sabbath ('sabbath' literally means 'stop'). Not in essence a spiritual day, but a day to stop from all work, to rest and to reconnect with God and with others.

> I find it fascinating that God took this so seriously that he enshrined it as one of the ten commandments.

We seem to take the other nine pretty seriously, but Sabbath in the 21st century seems like a bit of a joke, any sense of a day of rest replaced with shopping, DIY, paying bills, writing work emails and replacing one sort of work with another.

THE YEAR ➲ There was a rhythm to the year, marked by the seven feasts which were spread throughout the year. Times when the whole nation of Israel stopped, relaxed and feasted.

THE YEARS ➲ There was even a rhythm to the years, with a year of Jubilee every seven years where the land was rested, debts were cancelled and slaves were set free. And then every fifty years a double Jubilee.

REDISCOVERING RHYTHM

I haven't got this totally worked out, but I think there is something huge in us rediscovering the rhythm of life.

Finding again the rhythm of the day. Not answering email from the moment we wake up to the moment we go to sleep, but having times when we work and times when we rest and enjoy the day. Lingering over meals with family and friends, rather than rushing through them or eating them on our own in front of a TV. Spending more time interacting with the people around us rather than our 'friends' on Facebook and Twitter. Having not only a 'quiet time' in the morning, but regular moments throughout the day where we reconnect with God. And having a point in the day when we 'cross the line' and finish working, even if you're a busy mum with young children and you feel as though life is relentless.

Rediscovering Sabbath, not as some dull religious chore but as the gift of stopping, resting and refreshing our relationships with others and with God. Sabbath as a statement of trust in God, that it's OK that not everything on our to-do list has been done, and that our world won't fall apart just because we've stopped working.

Rediscovering the rhythm of the year. Not through a return to the Jewish feasts but through having regular times when we stop, take short breaks and holidays, where we do things we enjoy doing and refresh our bodies, our emotions and our souls.

And even rediscovering a rhythm to the years. Recognising the different seasons of life, and embracing them rather than resenting them. And perhaps not being afraid to take extended breaks every few years.

CHURCH IMPLICATIONS

All of this will have an impact not only on our individual lives but also on our lives as a church community. That means that we'll try to build rhythm into the life of the church.

Trying not to work volunteers and staff into the ground, but seeing them as people first. Being more interested in their physical, emotional and spiritual health than in the role they perform in the church. It means encouraging people and teaching on finding rhythm in all aspects of life, in the day, the week, the year and the years.

It means realising that for many Sunday is not a particularly restful day, and that some at least will need to find another day of the week to do Sabbath.

It also means that we'll recognise a rhythm to the life of the church. That there will be busy seasons – Christmas and Easter, the start of terms when lots of courses begin – and quieter times such as the summer holidays (although the exact reverse will be true for some ministries). We'll recognise this and plan the diary accordingly. For instance we don't usually meet on the Sunday after Christmas, simply to give everyone a chance to rest and to stop, and when we have a conference one Saturday we'll try to make sure the surrounding Saturdays are free.

SILENCE AND SOLITUDE

Tied in with this idea of rhythm is also, I believe, a need for us to rediscover patterns of silence and solitude. These things seemed to form part of the way Jesus lived, for instance we read:

> Very early in the morning, while it was still dark, Jesus got up, left the house and went off to a solitary place, where he prayed. (Mark 1:35)

This seems to have been a regular pattern in the life of Jesus, of getting away by himself to seek God. Yet the whole of our crazy 21st-century world seems to be pressing in the opposite direction. Even when we're on our own we want to be with people through Facebook and Twitter, and even when we're in silence we want to turn on a radio or TV, or put on headphones and listen to music or a podcast.

I've been thinking about the contents of this chapter for a number of years now, but only recently came across Peter Scazzero who leads a church in New York. He seems to be wrestling with many of the things I've talked about here but is much further down the road

SUGGESTED RESOURCES

of finding some answers than I am. I'd therefore encourage you to read anything that Pete and his wife Geri have written on this subject. This includes The Emotionally Healthy Church, Emotionally Healthy Spirituality, The Daily Office and I Quit.

Ordering Your Private World
Gordon MacDonald
A classic – a down-to-earth book on living life well.

**People were overwhelmed with amazement.
'He has done everything well,' they said.
'He even makes the deaf hear and the mute speak.'**

(Mark 7:37)

One of our core values is excellence, the desire to do things as well as we possibly can. We believe that excellence honours God and inspires people.

> First of all excellence honours God.

We serve a God who has done all things well. Who gave us the very best he had, his one and only son, so that we could come into a relationship with him. It therefore makes sense that we would want to do everything in life as well as we can to honour him. At work we should be the most diligent, resourceful, honest, reliable, joyful, dependable employees we can be – you don't honour God by turning up late every day! At home we should make sure the way we handle our finances, love our partners, raise our kids, entertain people in our homes and relate to our neighbours honours God. And in church life the quality of what we do and the diligence with which we do it should honour God.

> Secondly we know that excellence inspires people.

We don't mind people being offended by the gospel, by the message that Jesus Christ is the only way to get a relationship with God. But if they are going to be offended we want to make sure it's over the gospel and not how they were treated in the car park or greeted at the door, the terrible smell in the toilets or how out of tune the band were. In fact we want all those other things to have left such a positive impression on people that they will be much more open to the gospel than they might otherwise have been. The expectation of many people is that anything associated with church is going to be second-rate or shabby, which actually gives us a real opportunity to surprise them positively.

So what does excellence mean practically? Let's take a look at just a few areas

WELCOME

We want to strive for excellence in the way we welcome people. People will have made up their mind on what they think about our church community long before the preacher gets up to bring a message.

Their first impressions will often start with a visit to our website. We want to have a website which is welcoming but professional, where it's easy to find the information a first-time visitor might want and which gives a good flavour of the church. It also has to work as well on mobile phones as it does on a computer.

The same goes for any literature which goes to anyone other than regulars. No badly photocopied scraps of paper covered in word clip art (I do find it embarrassing that pizza delivery companies produce better literature than most churches); we want literature which will stand up against the very best of the world's creativity.

Then we want people to get a great physical welcome. To have the best parking spaces reserved for visitors, with all those regulars who are able prepared to walk a bit further. For them to be shown a parking space by a smiling car parker, and offered an umbrella if it's raining. To be greeted at the door by someone who is more interested in them than in their friend who has just walked in. If they've got children, to be taken to the kids' groups and helped to register them.

Then, when they get into the auditorium, to be chatted to by regulars. Not people on a specified welcome team, but just the folks around them who are friendly enough to break off chatting to their friends to say hello and introduce themselves.

BUILDINGS

We also want our buildings to speak of excellence. My experience is that most of us strive for excellence in our homes by making sure that they are clean, well looked after and welcoming. I don't believe that our church buildings should be any different.

The toilets should be clean and smell nice, the litter bins should be emptied whenever they get full, the rooms should be warm, the carpets and walls should be clean, there shouldn't be junk lying around, the light bulbs should all be working, the grass and hedges should be cut. Nothing we wouldn't do in our own homes, but somehow we can so easily apply a different standard to church.

All of this will cost money, whether we're in a building that we own or a rented facility, but it is a price worth paying.

MEETINGS

We want to produce meetings which are excellent too. That means they start and end on time.

That means that the band are chosen not only on how spiritual they are, but also on how well they can play and sing. It means the sound from the PA will be clear, the image on the screen will be bright and sharp and the platform will be well lit. It means that transitions between different elements of the meeting will have been thought through, that we won't use in-house language or jargon and will explain at each stage what we're doing. It means the people who speak from the platform will have the ability to speak in a way which engages people, have the right information, smile and know what is happening after them.

The same principles apply to all the courses and other gatherings being held in the name of the church.

EXCELLENCE IS EVERYONE'S RESPONSIBILITY

There's a danger in all this that we may think maintaining excellence is the responsibility of the people on duty, the welcomers, car parkers, kids' workers, musicians or whoever else it might be. But when guests come into my home I expect everyone in my family to take responsibility for them. We've taught our children that when visitors come we expect them to stop what they're doing, say hello and see if there is anything they can do to serve them. In the same way, when visitors come into God's house I believe that all of us who are part of the family have a responsibility to look out for them and care for them.

That means that if you see a new person who looks unsure of where to go, you help them find the kids' work and then help them find a seat. That if someone you don't recognise sits in the same row as you, you go and say hello to them. That if someone comes late into a meeting and the welcomer doesn't find them a seat, you take responsibility and find them a seat yourself, even putting out a new row if you need to. In any situation where a new person isn't being served well, you make it your responsibility to fix whatever the problem is. There may well be a problem there which in the longer term we need to look at and resolve, but the immediate issue is that someone new to us isn't being looked after well, and if you're part of the family, resolving that is part of your responsibility.

EXCELLENCE, NOT PERFECTION

We will never achieve perfection, not this side of heaven at least. There will always be something we could have done better, something we missed or overlooked, somebody who objected to something we said or did, somebody on the team who was just having a bad day or something we tried which didn't quite come off. The pursuit of perfection can rob us of our joy, and leave us feeling that we're never good enough.

Striving for perfection can also rob us of ever taking any risks. We must never be afraid of failure; in fact we need to embrace it because if we're not failing every now and again, we're probably not taking enough risks. Failure only becomes bad when we keep making the same mistake rather than learning from what went wrong and putting it right. So let's embrace a theology of failure which says that failure is not an option; it is a necessity if we are going to achieve all that God has called us to.

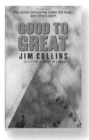

Good to Great
Jim Collins
In this fascinating book Jim Collins looks at some of the differences between good and great companies. It contains many insights which we can apply to church life.

SUGGESTED RESOURCES

It makes sense
     that we would want
          to do everything
in life as well as we can
          to honour him

MIKE

MIKE

Mike is a successful graphic designer with the likes of Miele, British Airways and Sony as past clients. He was drawn into a relationship with God via his son through music and worship. My childhood was defined by the death of my mum when I was nine years old. I was forced to grow up very quickly and help look after my little sister when my dad was working. My parents were Christians and we used to attend church on Sundays, but as my sister and I got older we began to lose interest and eventually stopped going. It wasn't that we didn't believe, we just didn't follow.

Every Christmas I went to church, and although I enjoyed the festive celebration it was never enough to make me want to go more regularly.

When I was sixteen years old I decided to move to London to find work, armed with just thirty quid and a mate's floor to sleep on. Fortunately, after a few disasters (including making myself homeless, jobless and hungry), the move was a success and I made my first steps into the publishing industry.

A few years later, broke and two stone lighter, I moved back to my dad's home in Berkshire and began a long career in everything from advertising and photography to newspaper publishing and production for TV and cinema. In 1987 I married Lorraine (we now have three grown-up kids) and started my own design business which really took off.

2008 was a turning point for me, when my son joined Kerith Community Church. At Christmas he suggested we went there with him. So we turned up at one of the events and I couldn't believe what I saw! With the large auditorium, the instruments and the lights I couldn't believe we were in a church, but what really hit me was the worship – it was just great to hear such lively worship in such a modern style. We liked it so much that we ended up coming back for more, and we were really impressed by how genuinely friendly everybody was – people were so welcoming and interested in who we were. I found myself wanting to learn more about Christianity and joined the Freedom in Christ course, which spurred me on to giving my life to God.

I've always believed that my creative talents are a gift from God and I've always wanted to give something back. I firmly believe that God put me on a path to the church that Christmas, and I've since gone on to help with things like promotional materials, banners and car park signs, postcards, stage set design, ministry logos and the website. I'm now Art Director for Kerith's LinK magazine.

My whole outlook has changed, and I feel as if I've been through a period of personal expansion. I'm less concerned about what people think – which allows me to be free in discussing my feelings and beliefs – and I find that God gives me confidence in all the different areas of my life, looking outward and not in.

artists

In the beginning God created...

(Genesis 1:1)

If all we had were these first five words of the Bible, then what we would know of the character of God would be that he is creative, that he is an entrepreneur who loves to innovate and produce new things. Please stop and think about that for a moment. We so often think of God as being solid, a rock, unchanging, the same yesterday, today and for ever. We can take great assurance and comfort from all of those truths, but sometimes we can forget that God is also creative. He loves to make new things, and then sit back and enjoy the thing he has just created.

Seven times in the Genesis 1 account of creation we are told that God stopped, looked at what he had done and 'saw that it was good'. There's almost a playfulness about God as this creative side of his character is expressed.

So often it seems to me in church we love to celebrate the fixed, solid, unchanging side of God's character. But the creative playful side can seem to get lost somewhere. I meet people who love old hymns and speak disparagingly of all the new songs. Yet they don't realise that many of the hymn writers were driven out of their churches for introducing such terrible new songs which didn't make use of the 'proper' instruments. Or how about people who love the King James translation of the Bible because of its old-fashioned language, forgetting that when it was translated it caused a spiritual revolution because it used the everyday language of the people of the day?

We want to take hold of both. We want to recognise what has gone before, honour it and where appropriate make use of it. But we must never do that at the expense of creativity, of grasping what is new, of taking hold of fresh ideas and new ways of doing things. As people created in the image of God we should be the most creative people on the planet. We should be known by what we are for and what we are innovating more than what we are against.

Here are a number of areas where we will seek to do that.

THE ARTS

There was a time when the greatest architects, composers and authors were nearly all found within churches. I believe that we've lost that ground to a fear and suspicion of the arts, terrified that we'll get contaminated if we step out into that world. Sadly others have moved in and taken the ground which by rights should be ours.

As a church we want to play our part in regaining some of that ground. That starts by celebrating the artists in our midst. Encouraging the musicians and songwriters by providing a place for them to hone their skills and sing their songs on Sundays, raising up the dancers and actors in our midst and giving them a platform to perform on, giving the video artists and movie makers the equipment they need, self-publishing the books of authors in our midst. Releasing the creativity in the young and in the old.

But ultimately we need our artists to **break out of the Christian bubble**. It isn't enough just to have new songs, even our songs, being sung at all the Christian events and conferences. Or to have our books being read by a Christian audience. They need to make their way into the mainstream, to go where pioneers like C.S. Lewis, Tolkien and U2 have gone before.

That can be a dangerous place, where we are open to broadsides from others in the Christian world, but it is a place where God wants us to go.

MORE THAN JUST THE ARTS

Let's be honest: there are lots of us who have almost no gifting when it comes to singing, playing an instrument, dancing, painting or acting (I speak as someone who was sacked from the worship group because of my lack of singing ability!). Because of that we can write ourselves off as not being creative. I simply don't believe that is true.

We are all created in the image of God, which means that all of us have a spark of creativity buried within us. We just need to realise that for different people that creativity will be expressed in different ways.

For me for years my creativity has been expressed through my 'other' job designing computer chips. Most recently I was a founding engineer at a company which makes high-speed servers, which have been used to make films such as Avatar. Now much of my creativity gets expressed through preaching, and steps such as writing this book.

For others it might be expressed through your job, DIY, gardening, restoring cars, building a business or any one of a myriad of other ways. We need to encourage everyone in our midst to go find their individual expression of creativity, and celebrate that, whatever it might be.

TECHNOLOGY

There have been times when the church has utterly grabbed the opportunity provided by new technology.

One of the reasons the early church grew so quickly was the transport network the Romans had developed. This allowed people to travel quickly and safely over large distances, and made it possible for Paul to establish a missionary strategy which required him to be very mobile.

Similarly the reformation moved at such a pace because people like Luther, Calvin and Tyndale grasped the opportunity to speak to the masses provided by the printing press. Christian entrepreneurs were at the forefront of setting up printing press companies to make use of this new technology.

And what of C.S. Lewis, who during the Second World War became the second most listened to voice on British radio after Winston Churchill, speaking hope and direction to the nation?

We are at the beginning of a similar technology breakthrough. Facebook, Twitter, blogs, Skype, Wikipedia, eBay, streaming media, podcasts, all of these are fundamentally changing the ways that people communicate, do business and spread information. We want to be at the forefront of working out how we can make the most effective use of all of this new technology.

This new technology is a great leveller. There was a time when if you were a musician, the only way you could get your music out was to get a recording contract. Now pretty much anyone can afford the tools required to record their music, and through YouTube get it to a potential audience of millions. There was a time when if you were an author, unless you had a publishing contract with a major publisher nobody would ever get to read your books. Now, with blogs and self-publishing, it is pretty much a level playing field for everyone. The same applies to people wanting to make short films. The equipment required to film and produce films used to cost millions of pounds, but it can now be done with very affordable PCs and cameras.

THINKERS

The world is desperately in need of Christians who will apply their brains, combined with their knowledge of God, to the great problems of our day. It sometimes seems that our emphasis on spiritual gifts has stopped us using our minds. We need to remember that for Joseph, though it was his spiritual gift of interpreting dreams that got him into Pharaoh's presence, it was his ability to strategise on how to overcome the forthcoming years of drought which got him to being number two to Pharaoh. It's not either/or but both. And we need to remember that for 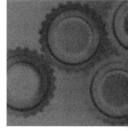 centuries the greatest scientific minds were in the church; in fact it was their belief in a God who had created a world with meaning and order which allowed people like Newton and Faraday to do the work they did, work which they saw as revealing the handiwork of God in nature.

We want to be part of raising up a new generation of great Christian thinkers in the worlds of science, education, health care, politics, law and many other areas. As we seek to restore and redeem what has been lost in the world, a key part of that will be thinking our way through some of the tough issues facing the world we live in, and bringing a godly, prophetic insight on them. Christians need to earn their place at the table of government not because we've had a part to play in the history of our nation, but because we've got something fresh, relevant, important and unique to say today.

Often this thinking will be on a local level. A school governor trying to think through how to move their school ahead. An administrator trying to improve the service offered by their doctors' surgery. But we also want to be making a difference nationally and internationally, to have thinkers at the highest levels.

ENTREPRENEURS

God's creativity was highly entrepreneurial. He created something out of nothing, something which had never existed before or previously been conceived. We need entrepreneurs both inside and outside the church, people who can birth new ministries, new companies, new charities and new social enterprises. This will mean taking risks with people.

UMBRELLAS

The church needs to be a safe place within which all these different expressions of creativity can flourish. I sometimes think of the church as being an umbrella, under which many different people can find the safe place, the encouragement, the direction, the inspiration and the leadership for their creativity to emerge.

Some of that will be within the limits of what defines church. Songs we sing, books we publish, ministries we launch and courses we run. But much of it will never have a church badge attached to it. Bands playing in local pubs, charities being headed up by church people, businesses being started by people in the church. It won't be church, but it will indirectly be church as it flows out of who we are as a community.

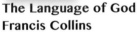

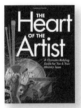

The Heart of the Artist
Rory Noland
A brilliant book on how creative people can find their place within the church.

SUGGESTED RESOURCES

The Language of God
Francis Collins
Written by the scientist who headed up the human genome project; he talks very personally on how we can find the wonder of God through modern science.

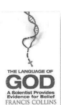

www.rzim.org
This is the website of Ravia Zacharias International Ministries. It is billed as 'helping the thinker believe, helping the believer think' and is a great example of what I've said about raising up a generation of Christian thinkers.

Purple Cow
Seth Godin
Not only a great example of what ideas presented creatively can look like, but also full of ideas on how we need to be exceptional in order to stand out in the world.

in the beginning

DAVE

Growing up as a teenager Dave had hopes and dreams about what he wanted to achieve in life. None of these seemed realistic, but since becoming a Christian he's seen God provide in the most amazing ways. When I left school in the summer of 2007, I was excited about what the future would hold. Having a place at the Academy of Contemporary Music in Guildford, I dreamt of a career as a professional musician. However just months after starting my course I was lonely and couldn't ignore the feelings of isolation. Then one day I bumped into my schoolmate Hudson's dad. He invited me to come and see his son's band 'Ethos' play at the Kerith Centre. I jumped at the chance of seeing my old friend.

I knew the Kerith Centre was a church and was sceptical about Ethos being a 'Christian band', but I was keen to catch up with my mate so I decided to go along. In the end I was totally blown away by the music they played. I was expecting to hear hymns and outdated songs, but I was really surprised that it was actually songs I really liked. When Hudson and I met weeks later, we talked about church, and about evolution, sex before marriage and all the things that for me meant religion and faith were out of the question. I began the conversation believing that there was definitely no God, but left it thinking that just maybe there was.

I was keen to find out more, and also looking to gain musical experience, so I found myself offering to help Ethos out during rehearsals. That ultimately led to my life-changing encounter with God.

Ethos were going to be playing at RockNations 2008, a Christian youth conference in Bradford, and they invited me to go with them. On the way up there I said to Lee (then Kerith's youth pastor) that I didn't think it was going to be my kind of thing, but he told me he had a feeling God would move powerfully in me that week, and he did! On the first night I encountered God in a big way and he gave me pictures of what I was going to be doing for him in the future. It was then that I decided to follow Christ.

So many things have changed since I became a Christian, particularly the way I treat people and the way I react to situations. I was never an angry person but I don't get frustrated or retaliate in the same way I used to. I now have so many loyal, true friends and I've learnt so much from being around some amazing people.

I always dreamt of playing in bands that travelled internationally. I wanted to write songs and teach music and manage other bands. I thought that being a Christian would mean having to give up these dreams, but when I decided to follow God he gave me a vision of these things actually happening in my life.

Now God has provided me with all the things I wanted to do – playing abroad as part of a band, training and mentoring Kerith's youth band Revolution, writing songs that have been sung in church, and teaching music through Kerith Worship Academy. Through being involved in both worship and the youth setup at the church it is a real privilege to see so many people's lives changed as mine has been changed.

EXCELLENCE IS EVERYONE'S RESPONSIBILITY

LET'S EXCEL

THREE

Vision for
the Future

history

In the future, when your children ask you, 'What do these stones mean?' tell them that the flow of the Jordan was cut off before the ark of the covenant of the LORD. When it crossed the Jordan, the waters of the Jordan were cut off. These stones are to be a memorial to the people of Israel for ever.

(Joshua 4:6–7)

Before we look at our vision for the future I want to take a moment to go over some of our history. History is important. Understanding history increases our confidence in God as we see how he has worked in the past. Understanding history allows us to honour those who have gone before and to recognise the contribution of previous generations. And understanding history allows us to avoid making the same mistakes over and over again and to learn from the past.

Here are some of the key dates in the history of our community:

1881 — Bracknell Baptist Church was started by a small community of believers, meeting in a Reading Room. The church later became part of the Baptist Union of Great Britain & Northern Ireland.

1892 — The first church building was opened in the centre of what was then the village of Bracknell. The site is now buried underneath a multi-storey car park!

1964 Ben Davies became the first full-time leader of Bracknell Baptist Church. This was one of the most important moments in our history. In the forty-three years Ben led the church, he took it from a very small church of about twenty people into one with national and international impact. We transitioned from being a democratic group voting at church meetings to being leader-led. We became a Spirit filled, outward-looking church.

1968 As Bracknell New Town was developed, the original church building was demolished and the Bracknell Development Corporation gave us a new site (where K2 is now) plus £12,000 compensation. A new 150-seater building was constructed in Church Road at a cost of £23,000. It was a radical design and thrust us into the 20th century!

1970s Under Ben's leadership, numbers grew as the church reached out into the community. We held open-air meetings at Bracknell town centre bandstand, became involved in annual town carnivals and started visiting door to door.
During this time the first housegroups were started, meeting in homes to worship and pray and care for one another. We held lunchtime meetings on Tuesdays for people working locally. On Sundays, worship gradually changed to include modern songs as well as hymns, and we began using other instruments as well as the organ. Increasing amounts of money were given away locally. The church was constantly evolving.

1980s Under Ben's leadership, the church outgrew the 'new' 1968 building and started to meet in a school hall on Sundays. We started to partner with the Newfrontiers family of churches. At the same time, the church set up a trust to buy more land on Church Road and began the project to build a 1,000-seat building. This era saw the start of our social justice ministry as we began a ministry for the deaf and hard of hearing. Our overseas involvement was also birthed as we started to invest leadership training and money in what is now a major church in Meru, Kenya.

1989 We moved into the Kerith Centre, built at a cost of £3.1 million (about £6 million in today's money), 98% of which came from church people. This was a remarkable achievement by a community of about 400 people in the middle of a recession, and made a national impact with coverage in the national press and on national TV. It was also done at a time when very few churches were embarking on major building projects. 10% of all the income was given away to other churches. **The name 'Kerith' came from 1 Kings 17:1–6 where God miraculously provides for Elijah in the Kerith ravine, and was chosen to represent God's miraculous provision of money to build the Kerith Centre.**

At the same time as moving into the Kerith Centre the name of the church was changed to Bracknell Family Church, better representing who we were.

1990s Having our own large building meant that we could reach many more people locally, nationally and internationally. Groups and courses like Sparklers (our parent and toddler group), Hilltop for adults with learning disabilities, Konnections for parents of children with special needs, the Alpha course and the marriage course all began. We started hosting conferences and events for wide-reaching organisations such as Willow Creek Association UK and Care for the Family. Local groups partnered with us; annual charity carol concerts were held with Bracknell Rotary Club for local primary schools to showcase their choirs.

1999 The 1968 church building was demolished and replaced with K2, a building for children, youth and the community, at a cost of £1.1 million.

2006 We opened a Christians Against Poverty centre, giving free debt advice. In the first five years over 500 people were helped and today we work with over a hundred households at any one time.

2007 In October I took over from Ben Davies as senior pastor. Today Ben continues to be an elder and a key part of our community.

2008 We changed our name to Kerith Community Church (we did think about being Kerith Family Church but weren't sure that being KFC was quite the image we wanted to project). Although we were happy to be Bracknell Family Church, the local community called us Kerith and we wanted to reflect that.

 2009 In January we changed from having different 10am and 6.30pm meetings on a Sunday to running the same meeting three times over at 9am, 11am and 7pm. In September we opened Bracknell Foodbank, which helped over 600 individuals or families in its first two years.

 Today Who we are today as a church community traces right back through all our history to the men and women of faith back in the 1880s. And we're making history now for the generations who will follow on from us. After looking back I want to be looking forward too, to where God wants to take us; that's what I'm going to talk about in the next chapter on vision.

One day we'll persuade Ben to write a history of his time as senior pastor; when he's done that we'll recommend here that everyone reads it!

SUGGESTED RESOURCES

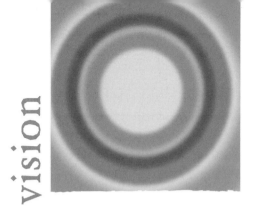

vision

Therefore go and make disciples of all nations, baptising them in the name of the Father and of the Son and of the Holy Spirit, and teaching them to obey everything I have commanded you.

(Matthew 28:19–20)

'Love the Lord your God with all your heart and with all your soul and with all your strength and with all your mind'; and, 'Love your neighbour as yourself.'

(Luke 10:27)

I often meet people who struggle with finding the will of God for their lives. They are like a sailing boat which is becalmed, sitting around waiting for God to tell them what to do and where to go. Often they are scared actually to do anything, worried that if they do the wrong thing they might step outside of the 'will of God' and get into all sorts of trouble.

I don't believe that God wants finding his will for our lives to be complicated, or something which drive us to inaction. As I look at the Bible it seems that God has a two-step approach to leading and guiding us: the big picture and the next step.

BIG PICTURE

First of all when God wants to guide us he gives us a big picture, a vision of where he wants to take us. That picture may be incredibly vague, may seem very fuzzy and be more of an impression than a clearly defined picture, but it's a vision which produces a sense of excitement, of purpose, of direction and of passion and a vision for which we'd be willing to sacrifice and suffer: what Bill Hybels describes as 'a picture of the future that produces passion'.[164]

On a personal note, what do you do if you don't have a vision for your life? Well, first of all, align yourself with God's overall vision for your life with the ideas I've laid out here. Join a local church, go on a Sunday, get into a small group community, serve, give your money, reach out to lost people around you, get involved in social justice, develop your personal relationship with God. Then find someone else who does have a vision and tuck yourself in behind their vision, be a part of what they're doing. Then seek God for his vision for your life. Seek God in prayer and fasting, immerse yourself in God.

Our vision as a church comes from a time in the 1980s when the elders sought God. They came up with our vision statement, which is:

To be a rapidly growing community of followers of Jesus Christ, contributing to local, national and international life.

There are five elements to this vision, which align with the five purposes Rick Warren identifies in his book The Purpose Driven Church. These are:

worship Jesus Christ and following him are at the core of who we are and what we do.

community We aren't just an organisation or a charity, we're a family and we want to grow in our friendships, relationships and care for one another.

evangelism Our vision is to grow rapidly as a result of lost people finding Christ, and for that message of Christ to be declared not just locally but nationally and internationally too.

discipleship We not only want to grow rapidly numerically but also to be rapidly growing in our relationship with Christ and in the fruit of the Spirit demonstrated in our lives.

social justice We seek to demonstrate practically the love of Christ locally, nationally and internationally.

Everything we do as a church should be covered by one of those five purposes.

You might also want to know what my personal vision is for us as a community. I've only had one occasion when I feel God has spoken to me directly. It came at a Bible week in a place called Stoneleigh near Coventry. The sermon that night was on people who had once felt they had had a vision from God, but for whom that vision had died. I was telling God that I felt like I'd never had my own vision but had just tucked in behind other people's visions. Well, that night God spoke to me in what I can only describe as an audible voice saying:

'You will lead churches of thousands.'

That's now my vision. First of all to see Kerith grow to be a church of thousands. Then to plant other churches which will grow to be churches of thousands. But for each to be a church which all the time embraces the five purposes we've identified for Kerith.

So how are we going to see these visions fulfilled? We'll look at that now.

NEXT STEPS

As well as giving us a big picture God will show us the next step towards making the big picture a reality.

Very often we would like God to show us all the steps to get to the goal, and we even try to formalise that by having five-year and ten-year plans laying out in incredible detail what we think is going to happen every year. But my experience is that God only ever shows us the next step towards fulfilling the vision.

Consider Abraham. God first of all gives him the big picture, the vision of the promised land, this place where they can build a nation and from which all the nations on the earth can be blessed. And then God simply tells him to go. No idea where he's going, just pack up all your stuff, uproot all your family and go to a land I will show you. [165] Or think of Jesus as he's about to leave the disciples and ascend into heaven. The big picture vision is to make disciples of all nations. A pretty big vision for this ragtag group of people. Yet what is the plan for them to fulfil the vision? Stay in Jerusalem and wait for the Holy Spirit to come. Nothing more. No idea of what lies beyond that. Just wait, and once the Holy Spirit comes I'll show you the next step. [166]

So our leadership teams are constantly seeking God for the next step. Sometimes that step is just the next logical thing to do, sometimes it comes through prophetic input, sometimes it comes from someone outside our community and sometimes it's forced on us by external circumstances. Whatever the step is, we'll look to take it as quickly and as purposefully as we can, and then begin to look for the next one. Often the next step is only revealed as we take the preceding one.

In the last few years there have been a number of next steps. Going to three meetings on a Sunday, redeveloping reception, changing the role of elders, various key staff appointments, re-shaping our small groups.

As for what's coming next – I have little idea! When and where will we do our next church plant? No idea! What will we do once we've grown in Bracknell to 2,000? Don't know! What will we do once the project in Serenje has been completed? Not a clue!

But I'm confident that, both personally and as a community, if we keep taking those next steps, God will take us to places far beyond anything we could ever ask or imagine.

The Purpose Driven Church
Rick Warren

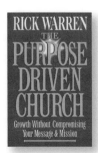

This book describes in much more detail the five purposes I have mentioned above, and is an excellent analysis of what it takes to build a great 21st-century church.

partnership

> In all my prayers for all of you, I always pray with joy because of your partnership in the gospel from the first day until now, being confident of this, that he who began a good work in you will carry it on to completion until the day of Christ Jesus.

(Philippians 1:4–6)

Hopefully by now you've realised that we want to make it very easy for people to feel a sense of belonging to our community. That everyone is welcome to come in, come on a Sunday, get involved in small group communities or go on a course, experience what it means to be a part of our community. In essence we want that aspect of our community to be like the flesh of the peach.

But we must always remember that the peach also has a core. For us that means that there will always be a group of people who represent the core of all that our church community is about, and who are totally committed to what we represent and stand for. By and large our leadership will be drawn from this core, our biggest givers in terms of both time and finances are likely to be in this core and those who will keep going even if the going gets tough will hopefully be this core.

We see this in the community of Jesus. There were all sorts of people who were associated with Jesus, who followed him and hung around with him. But he wasn't afraid to identify the core; he had the seventy-two,[167] the twelve [168] and the three.[169] On occasions he would gather these different groups and share specific teaching, leadership responsibilities and insights with them alone.

We feel that it's important for us to be able to identify our core too. We've decided to call those people who have chosen to identify with the core 'partners', and to set up a partnership programme so that they have a way of expressing their desire to be part of the core.

Before we dive into the detail it's worth saying that at the time of writing this book we haven't actually put any of this into practice! Thus it is quite likely that all of this will change as we actually look to implement these ideas – that's where the next issue of the book will come in!

WHY NOT MEMBERSHIP?

Some will ask the question 'why partners and not members?' Good question. I have a couple of answers and you'll have to judge whether they're as good as the question!

First of all I think that in our culture the idea of membership has been devalued. We become a member of something because of what we are going to get out of it. We become members of the RAC so they'll tow our car home if we break down. We become members of Blockbusters so we can rent DVDs. We become members of the National Trust so we can get into stately homes more cheaply. It's a lot about getting and very little about giving: almost the opposite of what we are trying to express. It seems to me that in many church settings membership implies little more than an agreement with the doctrinal position of the church. We want partnership to be about a much bigger commitment that that.

In contrast I think that partnership is a concept which resonates in our culture. Companies such as John Lewis refer to their staff as partners; that implies a much higher level of ownership than simply being an employee.

Secondly, membership can imply being in or out – which is something we strongly want to avoid. Yes, people are closer to or further from the core, and partnership is one of the ways by which we can define who is at the core, but you can belong without having to be a partner. Membership seems to imply a much stronger sense of being in or out than partnership does – to me at least.

However, this isn't a hill we're going to die on. If you want to think of partnership as membership then that's fine by us.

WHAT IS ASKED OF A PARTNER?

These are the things which we'll ask you to commit to if you want to become a partner:

- ⮑ Be a follower of Jesus Christ
- ⮑ Be baptised by full immersion in water
- ⮑ Have read or listened to the peach and coconut material and be happy to sign up to the culture, vision and values which it describes
- ⮑ Live a Christ-honouring lifestyle
- ⮑ Be a regular financial giver – moving beyond tithing
- ⮑ Volunteer in the life of the church
- ⮑ Regularly attend Sunday meetings, prayer meetings and partners' vision nights, and take part in a small group community. In all of these gatherings, you would get there on time and view yourself as a host in the house rather than a guest to be looked after
- ⮑ Be willing to be under the authority of and in good relationship with the leadership
- ⮑ Represent the church well in the wider community

WHAT DO I GET IN RETURN?

In outline, you get to be closer to the core – to know that you're not just a consumer of the church, but that you've chosen to give yourself to building the kingdom through the life of the church. That will mean invites to partners' evenings and access to the partners' blog where we'll talk in detail about future plans and ideas, and giving input in shaping and forming them before they are announced to the wider church. It also means the possibility of taking on significant leadership roles within the church, as we would only expect those to be open to people who have committed themselves to being part of the core.

There is also the sense that in your committing yourself to being part of the core, the leadership gain a greater freedom to speak into and shape your life, not in some weird, intrusive way, but simply as the fruit of your having committed yourself to the community and enjoying your relationship with it at a deeper level.

WHAT IS THE PROCESS?

As I've already said, the whole of this partnership process is a new idea for us, and at the time of writing this it's only an idea rather than something we've actually put in place. It may therefore all change, but for now this is how we envisage the process of becoming a partner working:

- ⮑ First of all come and be a part of our community. This isn't something we'd want you to do from a distance; we want you to have experienced what we're about for yourself. So come and join us on a Sunday, get into a small group community, feel from the inside what we're all about.

⊃ Then read this book or listen to the audio version and make a note of anything you're not sure about, don't understand or don't agree with.

⊃ Then go to the website (www.kerith.co.uk) and sign up to meet with one of our leadership team. This will be a chance to get to know them and for them to get to know you, for them to ask you some questions around the requirements for partnership and for you to ask any questions you might have.

⊃ If that goes well and you still want to become a partner, then come to an informal event hosted by Catrina and me so that we can have a chance to meet you and you can see what we're really like :)

PARTNERS FOR LIFE?

One of the issues we had in the days when we did have membership was that the list of members quickly became out of date. We are proposing that partnership would be an annual commitment, so once a year we will have a chat to check that you are still happy to continue being a partner. This will also be an opportunity for you to raise any issues or concerns you may have, and to talk about any serving opportunities, training or small group options you might want to explore.

Again as this whole partnership process is only a concept at the time of writing the book this may all change!

Read this book, ponder on it and think about whether you want to be a part of creating the sort of community it is talking about. If you do then consider signing up to the partnership programme.

SUGGESTED RESOURCES

Consumer or Consumed?
Charlotte Scanlon-Gambill
Charlotte very eloquently expresses the difference in attitude between those who are on the fringes of the church, the consumers, and those who are at the core, the consumed.

references

1 Coconuts
1 Mark 1:17
2 Acts 10:9-23
3 Acts 10:24-47
4 Galatians 2:11-13

2 Peaches
5 John 4:1–42
6 Luke 19:1–10
7 Luke 18:35–43
8 Matthew 8:1–4
9 Luke 7:36–50
10 John 2:1–11
11 Keller, Timothy,
The Prodigal God,
Hodder & Stoughton
2009, p.16
12 Luke 19:7
13 John 8:1–11
14 Burke, John,
No Perfect People Allowed,
Zondervan 2007, p.102
15 1 Corinthians 9:22
16 Acts 17:16–32
17 1 Corinthians 14

3 Core
18 Genesis 1–3
19 Revelation 3:20
20 Ephesians 1:4
21 Matthew 6:10

4 Flesh
22 Yancey, Philip,
What's So Amazing About
Grace?,
Zondervan 1997, p.11
23 John 3:21

5 Grace & Truth
24 Matthew 16:18
25 John 21:15–19
26 Staub, Dick,
The Culturally Savvy Christian,
John Wiley & Sons 2008,
pp.117–118

7 Unmasked
27 Keller, Timothy,
The Reason for God, Hodder &
Stoughton 2009, pp.xvi–xvii
28 John 16:33
29 John 11:35
30 Philippians 4:12
31 1 Timothy 5:23
32 Romans 12:15

8 Supernatural Soil
33 Mark 4:1–20
34 Psalm 127:1
35 Acts 3:1-16
36 Acts 10:44–48
37 Acts 28:1–6
38 Acts 28:7–10
39 Matthew 6:10

9 Treasure
40 Luke 15:4–7
41 Luke 15:8–10
42 Luke 15:11–32
43 Luke 19:10

10 Community
44 Hybels, Bill,
Building a Church of Small
Groups, Zondervan 2001, p.59
45 Lewis, C.S., The Four Loves,
Harcourt Brace Jovanovich
1960, p.169
46 John 17:23

11 Conflict
47 Genesis 3:12
48 Luke 19:45–46
49 Ephesians 4:26

13 Prayer
50 Acts 1:14
51 Acts 2:42
52 Acts 3:1-10
53 Acts 4.23-31
54 Acts 6.1-6
55 Acts 9:11
56 Acts 10, see verse 9
57 Acts 12.1-18, see verse 12
58 Matthew 6:17
59 Isaiah 58:6

14 Justice
60 Keller, Timothy,
quoted in Starke, John, 'What Does
Justification Have to Do with
Justice?', The Gospel Coalition,
http://thegospelcoalition.org/blogs/
tgc/2011/09/29/justification-and-
justice/, accessed May 2012
61 Matthew 22:37–39
62 Deuteronomy 15:4
63 Luke 10:25–37

15 Nations
64 Hybels, Bill, Just Walk Across the
Room, Zondervan 2006

16 Money
65 Matthew 17:27
66 Luke 18:22
67 John 12:4–6
68 Matthew 6:19–21
69 Luke 16:13
70 Acts 20:35
71 Luke 3:7–14
72 Mark 10:21
73 Luke 19:8
74 Acts 2:45
75 Acts 5:1–11
76 Acts 19:19
77 1 Timothy 6:10
78 1 Timothy 4:4–5
79 Luke 16:9
80 Psalm 1:3
81 2 Corinthians 9:6
82 Romans 13.8

17 Tithing
83 Numbers 18:21
84 Deuteronomy 12:17–18
85 Deuteronomy 14:28–29
86 Malachi 3:8–10
87 Matthew 5:17–20
88 McManus, Erwin,
An Unstoppable Force,
Flagship Church Resources 2001,
pp.204–205
89 Study Bible: English Standard
Version (ESV), Crossway 2008,
Kindle edition
90 Hebrews 11:6
91 Batterson, Mark,
Wild Goose Chase, WaterBrook
Multnomah 2008, p.86
92 2 Corinthians 9:7
93 1 Corinthians 16:2
94 1 Corinthians 16:2
95 2 Corinthians 8:2–3
96 Mark 12:44

18 Sex and the Peach
97 John 3:17
98 John 8:1-11
99 Luke 7:36–50
100 John 4:1-42
101 Genesis 38
102 Joshua 2:1–7
103 2 Samuel 11
104 Wilcock, Michael,
The Message of Luke,
IVP New Edition 1998, p.90

19 Sex and the Core
105 Song of Solomon 4:5
106 Chapman, Gary,
Making Love, Tyndale House
Publishers 2008, p.5
107 Genesis 2:24–25
108 Chapman, Gary,
Making Love, Tyndale House
Publishers 2008, p.3
109 1 Corinthians 6:16
110 Burke, John,
No Perfect People Allowed,
Zondervan 2007, p.227

20 Leadership
111 Exodus 18:13–27
112 Acts 6:1–7
113 Judges 4–5
114 Luke 4:1
115 Luke 4:14
116 Galatians 5:22–23
117 1 Samuel 14

21 Empowerment
118 Acts 9:26–28
119 Acts 11:25–26
120 2 Timothy 4:11

24 Baptism
121 Matthew 3:13
122 Matthew 28:19
123 Acts 2:41
124 Acts 8:12
125 Acts 8:36
126 Acts 9:18
127 Acts 10:48
128 Acts 16:15
129 Acts 16:33
130 Acts 18:8
131 Acts 19:5
132 Luke 23:43
133 Acts 2:41
134 Titus 3:5
135 Acts 2:38

25 Communion
136 Revelation 19:9

26 Spirit Filled
137 John 16:7
138 Acts 2:1–41
139 Exodus 31:1–3
140 Judges 13:24–25
141 Judges 6:34
142 1 Peter 2:9
143 Matthew 1:18
144 Luke 1:15
145 Luke 3:22
146 Luke 4:1
147 Luke 4:14
148 Acts 2:4
149 Acts 10:44–46
150 Acts 10:47
151 Acts 9:17
152 Acts 19:1-2
153 Acts 19:2
154 Luke 11:9–13
155 Galatians 5:22–23
156 1 Corinthians 13
157 1 Corinthians 12:27–31

27 Spirit Filled Peaches
158 1 Corinthians 14:18
159 1 Thessalonians 5:20
160 Study Bible: English Standard
Version (ESV), Crossway 2008,
Kindle edition

28 Wolves
161 Galatians 5:22–23
162 1 Corinthians 14:29
163 1 Corinthians 13:9

33 Vision
164 Hybels, Bill,
Courageous Leadership,
Zondervan 2002, p.32
165 Genesis 12:1-3
166 Luke 24:46-49

34 Partnership
167 Luke 10:1
168 Luke 6:13
169 Luke 9:28

BOOKS RECOMMENDED
IN THE PEACH & THE COCONUT

Title	Author	Publisher	ISBN
Unstoppable Force	Erwin Raphael McManus	Flagship Church Resources	978-0764423062
No Perfect People Allowed	John Burke	Zondervan	978-0310275015
The Prodigal God	Timothy Keller	Hodder & Stoughton	978-0340979983
Vintage Jesus	Mark Driscoll & Gerry Breshears	Crossway	978-1433519659
The Lion, the Witch and the Wardrobe	C. S. Lewis	Harper Collins	978-0007115617
What's So Amazing About Grace?	Philip Yancey	Zondervan	978-0310245650
The Culturally Savvy Christian	Dick Staub	John Wiley & Sons	978-0470344033
The Barbarian Way	Erwin Raphael McManus	Thomas Nelson Publishers	978-0785264323
The Reason for God	Timothy Keller	Hodder & Stoughton	978-0340979334
God on Mute	Pete Greig	Kingsway Publications	978-1842913178
In a Pit with a Lion on a Snowy Day	Mark Batterson	Multnomah Press	978-1590527153
Sun Stand Still	Steven Furtick	Multnomah	978-1601423221
Just Walk Across the Room	Bill Hybels	Zondervan	978-0310272182
Making Small Groups Work	Dr Henry Cloud & Dr John Townsend	Zondervan	978-0310250289
Everybody's Normal Till You Get to Know Them	John Ortberg	Zondervan	978-0310228646
The Peacemaker	Ken Sande	Baker Books	978-0801064852
Men are from Mars, Women are from Venus	John Gray	Harper Element	978-0007152599
How to Read the Bible for All Its Worth	Gordon D. Fee & Douglas Stuart	Zondervan	978-0310246046
Study Bible	English Standard Version (ESV)	Crossway	978-0007237142
Prayer That Brings Revival	David Yonggi Cho	Charisma House	978-0884195801
Too Busy Not to Pray	Bill Hybels	IVP	978-1844745098
Prayer	Richard Foster	Hodder & Stoughton	978-0340979273
Generous Justice	Timothy Keller	Hodder & Stoughton	978-0340995099
Nevertheless	John Kirkby	Christians Against Poverty Books	978-0954641047

SUGGESTED RESOURCES

Title	Author	Publisher	ISBN
Money, Possessions and Eternity	Randy Alcorn	Tyndale House Publishers	978-0842353601
The Gift of Giving	R. T. Kendall	Hodder & Stoughton	978-0340863312
Making Love	Gary Chapman	Tyndale House Publishers	978-1414300184
Courageous Leadership	Bill Hybels	Zondervan	978-0310248811
Axiom	Bill Hybels	Zondervan	978-0310282594
Humilitas	John Dickson	Zondervan	978-0310328629
Biblical Eldership	Alexander Strauch	Distributed by Dayspring	978-0936083117
The Starfish and the Spider	Ori Brafman & Rod A. Beckstrom	Portfolio	978-1591841838
Good to Grow	Steve Tibbert	Authentic Media	978-1860248122
Letters Across the Divide	David Anderson and Brent Zuercher	Baker Publishing Group	978-0801063435
Who Stole My Church	Gordon MacDonald	Nelson	978-0785230496
Systematic Theology	Wayne Grudem	IVP	978-0851106526
Questions of Life	Nicky Gumbel	Alpha International 2010	978-1905887828
Joy Unspeakable	D. Martyn Lloyd-Jones	Kingsway	978-1842913956
Surprised by the Voice of God	Jack Deere	Kingsway Publications	978-1842912850
The Emotionally Healthy Church	Peter Scazzero	Zondervan	978-0310293354
Emotionally Healthy Spirituality	Peter Scazzero	Thomas Nelson	978-0849946424
The Daily Office	Peter Scazzero	Willow	978-0744198713
I Quit	Geri Scazzero	Zondervan	978-0310321965
Ordering Your Private World	Gordon MacDonald	Highland Books	978-1897913673
Good to Great	Jim Collins	Random House Business	978-0712676090
The Heart of the Artist	Rory Noland	Zondervan	978-0310224716
The Language of God	Francis Collins	Pocket Books	978-1847390929
Purple Cow	Seth Godin	Penguin	978-0141016405
The Purpose Driven Church	Rick Warren	Zondervan	978-0310208136
Consumer or Consumed	Charlotte Scanlon-Gambill	Abundant Life Publishing	978-0953851621

The Peach & the Coconut is also available on-line as an e-book, and in an audio version which you can access via the Kerith website (www.kerith.co.uk) either as a download or by ordering a memory stick.

You can follow Simon via his blog:
www.simonbenham.com
and his Twitter:
@simonbenham